Revised and
Expanded Edition

the freelance academic

reclaim your career, creativity, and mental health

THE FREELANCE ACADEMIC

Reclaim Your Career, Creativity, and Mental Health

KATIE ROSE GUEST PRYAL

Blue Osprey Books

Copyright © 2025 by Katie Rose Guest Pryal

All rights reserved.

No part of this book may be reproduced in any form or by any electronic or mechanical means, including information storage and retrieval systems, without written permission from the author, except for the use of brief quotations in a book review and as permitted by copyright law.

Pryal, Katie Rose Guest. 1976-.

The Freelance Academic: Reclaim Your Career, Creativity, and Mental Health, Revised and Expanded Edition.

ISBN Paper: 978-1-947834-95-8

ISBN Ebook: 978-1-947834-94-1

1. Education, Higher. 2. College Teachers. 3. Careers. I. Title.

814'.6

First Blue Osprey Books edition, 2025.

Revised and expanded edition published in 2024 by Blue Crow Books.

First edition published in 2019 by Blue Crow Books.

Blue Osprey Books

Published by Blue Osprey Books,
a division of Pryal Consulting, Inc.
Chapel Hill, NC
blueospreybooks.com
Cover Design by Lauren Faulkenberry

Disclaimer

This book is sold with the understanding that neither the author nor the publisher is providing legal, investment, accounting, or other professional services.

While the publisher and author have used their best efforts in preparing this book, they make no representations or warranties with respect to the accuracy or completeness of its contents.

The advice and strategies contained in this book may not be suitable for your situation. You should consult a professional when appropriate.

Also by Katie Rose Guest Pryal

NOVELS

Entanglement

Chasing Chaos

Fallout Girl

Take Your Charming Somewhere Else

NONFICTION

Life of the Mind Interrupted: Essays on Mental Health and Disability in Higher Education

Even If You're Broken: Bodies, Boundaries, and Mental Health

A Light in the Tower: A New Reckoning with Mental Health in Higher Education

The Freelance Academic: Reclaim Your Career, Creativity, and Mental Health

Praise for LIFE OF THE MIND INTERRUPTED

Personal, political, polemical, and pointed in its vision for transforming higher education to be more inclusive of disabled and mentally ill people. If you want to understand how higher education is built, and not built, for people with disabilities—especially mental health–related ones—Pryal's book is for you.

Book Riot

Pryal writes with a refreshing and raw honesty. A must-read, not just for those in academia.

Booktrib Magazine

Pryal is one of the foremost writers of disability and higher education we have today.

Catherine Prendergast, author of ***The Gilded Edge: Two Audacious Women and the Cyanide Love Triangle That Shook America***

Pryal's wit and humor shine through even as she tackles harrowing subjects, like living with depression and suicide. This is not a book to miss.

Kelly J. Baker, award-winning author of ***Sexism Ed: Essays on Gender and Labor in Higher Education***

These thoughtfully chosen and arranged essays grapple with issues relevant to disabled students and scholars as well as those who would be allies.

Kecia Ali, author of **Human in Death: Morality and Mortality in J. D. Robb's Novels**

Praise for THE FREELANCE ACADEMIC

A piercing examination of how higher education institutions exploit adjunct faculty and untenured staff and a roadmap that's as practical as it is hopeful for anyone with an advanced degree wondering if there's a better way. (Spoiler alert: There is.)

Booktrib Magazine

Ultimately, Pryal's becomes both a cautionary tale and a beacon of hope for frustrated academics in similar positions. *The Freelance Academic* traces a path out of traditional academia with grace and humor.

Foreword Reviews

So many academics—current, former, and struggling—will see themselves in Pryal's story. I hope just as many see all of the possibilities she enumerates and understand, as she does, that the passions and talents that draw us to the university in the first place are often best used outside it.

Rebecca Schuman, author of ***Schadenfreude, A Love Story***

With candor and vulnerability, Pryal shares her own experiences and hard-fought wisdom to make a compelling case for a rewarding professional life beyond the walls of traditional academia.

Amy Impellizzeri, award-winning author of **Lawyer Interrupted: Successfully Transitioning from the Practice of Law—and Back Again**

An indictment of how the academy squanders talent by embracing the gig economy through contingent labor and the devaluation of teaching. A new, necessary book.

Catherine Prendergast, author of **The Gilded Edge: Two Audacious Women and the Cyanide Love Triangle That Shook America**

Praise for EVEN IF YOU'RE BROKEN

Pryal's book takes a significant place in the discussion, demanding to be seen and heard, giving a voice to survivors whose bravery is often overlooked just because they are silent.

Booktrib Magazine

A patchwork quilt of stories, raw emotion, and insights that will touch every reader. The result is moving, vital, and somehow hopeful for survivors and society both.

Washington Post bestselling author Kelly Harms

Rich in vulnerability and candor, Pryal's evocative essays remind us that the survivor journey is far from linear, and that there is power and beauty in our imperfect journey.

> Andrea Pino, co-author of **We Believe You: Survivors of Campus Sexual Assault Speak Out**

Pryal deftly unpacks the way both individuals and institutions fail survivors—and clearly explains how we can all do better.

> **Washington Post** bestselling author Camille Pagán

A harrowing, necessary, and beautiful book.

> Kelly J. Baker, award-winning author of **Sexism Ed: Essays on Gender and Labor in Academia**

For Michael, who helped me take the leap.
For my boys, who remind me what I'm working for.

Contents

Introduction to the Revised and Expanded Edition	xvii
Foreword	xxiii
Prologue: A Lecturer's Almanac	1

Part I
Coming to Be a Freelance Academic

1. A Manifesto for the Freelance Academic	13
2. What Does It Mean to Be a Freelance Academic?	22
3. On Not Writing *Job Insecurity, Anxiety, and Entering Public Life*	27
4. On Writing *Making Your Writing Matter*	35
5. Epiphany *The Burden of Creativity Falls to Us*	45
6. Negative Capability *Critiquing and Loving Higher Education*	50
7. Losing My Affiliation *How to Plan Ahead If You're Planning to Leave*	53
8. Reason to Believe *Setbacks Happen*	57
9. Bridging Academia *It Is Possible to Straddle Two Worlds*	60

Part II
Labor Conditions in Higher Education

10. Quit Lit Is About Labor Conditions	65
11. The University Is Just Another Client	71
12. The Ugly Side of Academia *It's not sour grapes. It's waking up.*	77
13. The Invisible Adjunct Hero at Kentucky *How Higher Ed Prizes Contingent Overwork*	81
14. The Racism False Equivalence Strikes Again *Public Engagement Is Risky for Vulnerable Faculty*	85
15. What's Your BATNA? *Finding Leverage in Negotiations*	90
16. Leaving a Legacy Off the Tenure Track	96

17. Why Attend Conferences as a Freelance Academic?	101
18. Why Am I Teaching Again?	105

Part III
Career Advice

19. Launch Your Career Like James Bond	111
20. How to Start Working for Yourself	115
21. How Can You Earn Money?	122
22. Run Your Business Like a Business	127
23. But I'm Still In Higher Ed *Tax Deductions for Contingent Faculty*	137
24. It's Not Personal. It's Strictly Business *Networking Advice*	142
25. Three Stories from Freelance Academics	149

Part IV
Writing for the Public

26. So You Want to Be a Freelance Writer	157
27. Ten Questions Every Academic Should Ask Before Writing for the Public	167
28. You Want to Write for the Public, but About What?	174
29. The Venue, the Pitch, and the Fee	179
30. Public Writing in Uncertain Times	185
31. How to Lose an Editor in Five Days	190
Epilogue: Finding Stability as a Freelance Academic	198
Notes	203
Acknowledgments	211
About the Author	213

Introduction to the Revised and Expanded Edition

Shortly after I left my full-time higher education teaching position, I tumbled into the darkest depression of my life. In the first edition of *The Freelance Academic*, I don't mention this period of depression, even though I was going through it while writing the book. One reason I kept my depression from the book is shame, which always makes mental health hard to talk about. I tried to keep up a good front because of my career change. But we cannot talk about leaving higher education without talking about mental health.

After leaving my job, my colleagues, and my routine, my mental health was a mess. But my mental health was a mess before I left, too, in part because I was in full burnout. As burnout expert Rebecca Pope-Ruark points out, "Burnout is endemic in higher education."[1] Burnout is rampant in academia because of institutional factors that push faculty to overwork themselves. As psychologists explain, "Academia needs to change in structural and cultural ways" if we hope to reduce burnout among faculty.[2] These structural changes must come from the top; they are not changes that individuals can make.

As Pope-Ruark writes, because her burnout was so awful and the untenable demands that caused it were not going to change, she left behind a tenure-track position for a contingent faculty position at a different institution. She is much happier now. But leaving to take a job with less prestige caused Pope-Ruark to feel ashamed. In fact, Pope-Ruark explains how the widespread adoption of contingent faculty jobs exacerbates the burnout problem because higher ed is "a system that persuades us that academia is a higher calling, that we are fortunate to have jobs when so many other smart, capable colleagues are scraping by in precarious adjunct roles, that our identities must revolve around our institutions and disciplines and that leaving higher ed is a failure of character." As Pope-Ruark attests, the fall from the tenure-track to a contingent job was a threat that kept her and her colleagues in line.

Tenure-track jobs harm mental health, but contingent jobs, for reasons I discuss in this book, are far more likely to do so. Indeed, my contingent career did harm my mental health. In retrospect, it is surprising that I didn't burn out sooner. I worked long hours doing repetitive tasks with no opportunity for advancement and little control over my work because I couldn't design my courses or teach any course beyond first-year writing. I was paid less than half of what my tenure-track colleagues were paid, and then these "colleagues" dismissed me because they considered my job inconsequential. Some ignored me, some dressed me down for various perceived slights, and one chased me out into the parking lot and yelled at me for being "rude" to her when I didn't greet her "properly." I walked on eggshells because I had no job security and therefore constantly feared that I would be fired. My career was in the hands of my students' course evaluations and those of my tenure-track colleagues who decided my fate yet disdained the work I did.

Because my mental health was failing, staying in this job was never an option. So, I listened to my body and left, I believed, before it was too late. But leaving didn't magically make me better. Shortly after I left, burnout developed into a serious depression. At the same time, I also experienced the sudden loss

Introduction to the Revised and Expanded Edition

of a small and supportive community of fellow contingent faculty colleagues. Losing this support system made rebuilding my mental health even more difficult.

Thus, I'm starting this introduction to this revised and expanded edition of *The Freelance Academic* with a discussion of mental health because I neglected its importance in the first edition of the book. You cannot make even minor decisions about your career without taking into account your mental well-being. And you definitely cannot make big ones.

Stepping back from academia can be excellent for your mental health. After my health improved, I reaped these benefits. For example, I was finally able to speak freely about my bipolar disorder after keeping it hidden my entire career. In one of my first public essays, I wrote about the shame I felt hiding the diagnosis from my colleagues for a decade.[3] It was wonderful to be able to publicly own my complete self without worrying whether I would be fired because of other people's ableism.

Plus, the stress of working as contingent faculty takes a vicious toll on our mental health. This stress must be part of the discussion when we make career decisions, especially given that three-quarters of higher education courses are taught by contingent faculty and over two-thirds of all faculty are contingent.[4] Thus, I'm writing this new edition, in part, because we must ask ourselves what we are trading when we choose to stay in higher education. We must talk about the low pay, the long hours, the repetitive classes, the mistreatment by our so-called colleagues. We must talk about the anxiety, chronic stress, burnout, and depression that research shows that the contingent faculty life often brings.[5]

A Note on Vocabulary

Allow me to clarify some terms that I use in this book whose meanings may be, for a variety of reasons, fuzzy.

Faculty. As I have written, when I use the term faculty, "I am referring to all higher education workers who educate...students, be they librarians, clinicians, academic support professionals, or classroom teachers."[6]

Tenure-track. When I refer to tenure-track faculty, I'm referring to all faculty on tenure lines, whether they are seeking tenure or already tenured. A tenure-track professor is hired on a probationary basis during which they have time to work to "gain tenure," usually seven years, although if they work fast, they can "go up for tenure" sooner. When a professor becomes "tenured," they have, essentially, permanent job security, so long as their institution is financially secure (so that their job can't be cut because of funding) and so long as they aren't fired for cause, which takes a whole lot. For example, sexual harassment of students is not enough to get a tenured professor fired.[7]

Contingent faculty. I use this term to refer to all faculty who work off of the tenure track. Terms that I include under this umbrella are "precarious faculty," "adjuncts," "adjunct professors," "contingent professors," and more.

Professor. Anyone who teaches in a classroom in higher education is a professor, whether contingent or tenure-track. To profess means to teach, and to withhold the title of "professor" simply because a professor is contingent is an institutional power game. In fact, as historian and higher ed critic Bret Devereux points out, "Unlike the tenure-track, where there is a clear progression of positions each with a standard title, NTT [non-tenure-track] positions are a confused jumble, often by design, with very different positions often sharing job titles."[8] Why would colleges use confusing job titles for contingent faculty? Devereux writes that we must "strongly suspect" that "this confusion is intentional, with universities and departments using job titles as a means to obfuscate just how much of their teachers are not permanent faculty."

Introduction to the Revised and Expanded Edition

Changes in this Edition

While there are many changes in this new edition that improve the book, at the same time the book remains the award-winning and useful book it has always been. The three main changes to the book are these:

First, as I mentioned above, I revised the book to bring to the forefront issues of mental health whenever they are relevant. Most of these revisions only required taking mental health discussions that were already there and giving them more airtime.

Second, I added five new chapters on writing for the public, which provide detailed guidance on a subject that many new freelance academics in all fields have expressed interest in. The inclusion of these new chapters required reorganization of the book, which now has four Parts instead of three.

Third, I changed how I provide resources to readers. At the end of the first edition was a short list of resources for aspiring freelance academics, which I have now removed because the data was woefully out of date. Additionally, the first edition included very few endnotes, instead using in-line journalism-style citations. In this edition, I added detailed endnotes that include hyperlinks so that you can find the resources yourself if you want to learn more.

Book Overview

This new edition features this Introduction, the Foreword, and the Prologue. It is then divided into four parts.

Part 1, "Coming to Be a Freelance Academic," provides advice on how to change your mindset to one of a freelance academic. It uses storytelling, in particular the story of how I left academia and decided to make a new career. You'll read about mistakes, failures, successes, epiphanies, things that worked, things that didn't, and everything you might want to know as you contemplate making a transition from higher education to a career outside of or adjacent to academia. As my friend Kelly J. Baker once told me, too many books and articles about alternative academic careers leave out the hard stuff. I'm leaving it in.

Part 2, "Labor Conditions in Higher Education," addresses the changing academic workplace, including job insecurity, low pay, long hours, heavy course loads, and everything else that make up the life of a contingent faculty member. This life is not what most of us were aiming for when we finished graduate school. Understanding the labor practices that undergird the modern university is essential to making the shift to being a freelance academic.

Part 3, "Career Advice," collects the most solid advice I can give to current and former faculty looking to make careers on their own terms as freelance academics, whether those careers mean leaving academia altogether or staying in and finding greater fulfillment by doing other work beyond their academic jobs.

Part 4, "Writing for the Public," gives practical advice for how to take your knowledge and your scholarship and turn it into writing you can do for popular audiences. It addresses why you might want to do this work, the benefits and risks, practical concerns such as how to interact with editors, and more.

Let's get started.

Foreword

BY KELLY J. BAKER

I am a freelance academic. And I have been for at least six years. I left my academic post, as a lecturer, in 2013, and I had no idea what I was going to do with my career or my life even. I floundered and flailed as I tried to figure out what I wanted to be when I grew up, except I was already a grown-up with two kids in tow and no idea how to shift to a career that wasn't an academic one. So, I started freelance writing, built on my academic work to become a (paid) public speaker, worked as a higher ed journalist, tried a lot of things that never panned out, and finally realized I had a talent for editing. (Who would have guessed that grading hundreds of undergraduate papers a semester would build my editing skills?)

I became a freelance academic, but the problem was I didn't know it. I described my career as "adjacent to academia," which explained how I positioned myself but not really what my career was. I didn't have the vocabulary to describe what my new career —outside the academy—fully entailed. I moved from graduate student to adjunct to full-time lecturer to part-time writer and stay-at-home mom. Then, I added gigs that included editing a magazine on higher education, writing nonfiction books that weren't academic monographs, developmental editing books for

Foreword

academics and memoirist. I dread pulling together a bio because there's not an elegant way to capture all the types of gigs that I do each year. I patch-worked a career, which appears more catch-all than consistent.

When I give the short version of what I do, I explain that I'm an editor, writer, and speaker with a religious Studies PhD. Try putting all of those on a business card or say them five times really fast. Instead, I have two business cards: one for my main gig as editor of *Women in Higher Education* and one for everything else. Somewhere in my office, the front room of my house really, there's a box with old business cards with a different title from my time in the ivory tower. Artifacts of the life I thought I would lead that never quite worked out.

I trained to be an academic. I ended up being something else entirely. It's taken me years to realize that I'm not alone. And you won't be either if you decide to step outside the academy and build a different career, a different life. Katie is here to help you, as she's helped me as a colleague and friend, to realize that it's okay to create your own career and show you how. It was more than okay to build a career that I wanted rather than the one everyone expected me to have. Just because I trained to be a scholar didn't mean I had to be one. I had more agency than I knew. I could and did master new skills. I could rely on what I learned in my PhD to do something different, terrifying and new. I could create a legacy to be proud of. I could do all those things if I just decided to.

You can do all those things too. You can be a freelance academic too, if you let Katie lead the way. And you should let her lead the way.

If you are picking up this book right now, you are already considering options beyond academic careers. (It's good to see what's out there.) Or maybe, you just want to see what the possibilities for your career might be. (Another good choice.) Or maybe, you just want a swift kick in the pants to convince you to make a change. (Which can also be good.)

Foreword

I'm happy to tell you, dear reader, that this book offers you all three.

Katie provides the how-tos of building your career as a freelance academic, explains the labor exploitation endemic to higher ed, and tells you what worked and what didn't for her.

One of the things I tend to hate, and I do mean hate, about these typical stories of transitions is that they are easy exit and entry stories. The person quits their academic post and then lands a new job, almost instantly. They are out of one career and then into another. Everything seems so damn easy. Nothing is bumpy, frustrating, or taxing. A can-do attitude is all you need. It's not though.

Part of the reason for my strong feelings about easy, frictionless stories is that they were antithetical to what I experienced. There was instant success. And here I was trudging and toiling with some wins but mostly I had a stack of rejections or, even worse, the radio silence that suggested I wasn't even worth responding to. If a résumé or pitch goes out into the world and no one responds, did you actually send it?

It was hard not to feel like a failure when all the advice suggested anyone could make the shift from academic work to alternative academic work. And yet, I wasn't a failure; those career transitions are hard. They take hard work, luck, energy, and time. Things often don't pan out, but sometimes, they do.

Katie's honesty about her own journey, then, is rare among the stories of transitions out of higher ed. You get to learn from her mistakes because she's brave enough to share them. You get the benefit of hard-learned lessons as well as realizing that failure teaches something important and is unavoidable. Learning from what doesn't work show us what does. Her advice is golden as she prods you to really think about the career you want and what it takes to make that happen.

As I was reading *The Freelance Academic*, I wished that I had had this book six years ago, so I would have felt like I could have pulled together a career outside of academia with a lot less anguish, sleepless nights, and utter terror.

So, reader, sit down and get comfy and be ready to take notes. This book is like a good coffee date with that friend who is kind (and maybe a little bit bossy). She's the friend that wants what is best for you, and she's determined to make that happen. She's guiding (maybe, prodding?) you to have the career and life you want. She's laying down the options and how to make them happen. Let Katie be that friend. Let her guide and advise you. Listen to what she has to say. And then, take the plunge. Build that career you want. Become a freelance academic. And never look back.

January 2019

Prologue: A Lecturer's Almanac

March 2007

THE HALL OF THE DEPARTMENT IS A 1960S-ERA BUNKER, MOLDED OF concrete and rebar, with tall, narrow windows to repel even the most determined activist. I watch my feet as I climb the linoleum-clad stairs so that I don't stumble in my skinny high heels, bought specifically to match this suit. The suit is black, with pale pinstripes, more fashionable than the interview suit.

After the years I'd spent working as a lawyer, I'd always sworn I would never buy one of those.

Dr. Composition and Dr. Rhetoric sit in a conference room. He's tenured and directs the first-year writing program; she's an assistant professor. I have a new doctorate in rhetoric and composition, the "most marketable" degree as everyone on my dissertation committee promised me. And it seems so, since Dr. Composition and Dr. Rhetoric want to hire me for this special position, crafted just for me or someone like me, for someone with special training in special disciplines, like law.

Plus, Dr. Composition says, it pays really well and comes with great research support. Sure it's still a contract position, but the contract is multi-year, and the Department Chair is really committed to changing the lecturer paradigm.

Dr. Composition says, when I ask about the possibility for contract renewal, "I promise we'll continue to exploit you as long as you let us."

Dr. Composition laughs at his joke. I smile to show I'm hip to the humor, but really, I don't understand what's so funny. Dr. Rhetoric looks uncomfortable, but she smiles in the way that women do when they know they must to keep the peace.

April 2007

I moved here for him, for Mr. Tall. Like many women before me, I traded some super-bright job offers for a pretty darn shiny one and a bungalow with the man I love.

In late April, I get a phone call from the chair of an English department in a city many states away. He's calling to offer me a position at his school, one I applied for months ago. I say I've taken a job at the Bunker, so I'm not available anymore.

He says, "I'm not surprised. Talent like yours gets snatched up quick."

When I hear his words, I feel a twinge, thinking maybe I've accepted a job that isn't good enough, that I should have held out for something better.

But I convince myself I'm satisfied. The job is a good one. Only six courses a year—a great course load for a lecturer. And the pay, it's not so bad. And isn't it more important to be near the person I care about most in the world? Would I really trade Mr. Tall for the tenure-track?

A few days later, Mr. Tall says he wants to take me to dinner near the Bunker. First, he suggests a walk around campus. He says, "I've always loved this place at dusk."

A decade ago, my new institution belonged to him, a skinny kid with big round glasses who came on a full scholarship. The coincidence across space and time suits my love of scientific anomalies. We stop outside my Bunker-to-be, and he pulls me into the foyer. We stop at the Board, with its black background and white letters, the long list of professors' last names with digits adjacent indicating the small rooms where genius happens.

"Your name will be up there soon," he says.

Outside, in the warm spring evening, he drops to a knee, holding something round and shiny. "Now you'll think of me every day when you come to work."

August 2007

The syllabi are written. The readings selected and scanned. The bus schedule memorized. The office keys placed on my keychain, the copy codes in my head. I am, I believe, ready.

My office, I discover, was painted pink and yellow, each wall a solid pane of color, by the graduate students who inhabited it before me. Pink paint splatters the ceiling and the baseboards, yellow drips have dried on the desks and linoleum. I hang my four diplomas, hoping to distract visitors from the unprofessional colors with my professional credentials.

I visit Dr. Rhetoric's office, professionally painted a refreshing spring green. She reassures me that the department pays to repaint offices. "You just have to ask," she says.

A few days later, I request a repainting. I learn that, because I am a lecturer, the department will not pay to repaint my office.

Every time a student comes for office hours, there's a funny moment when the shocking colors evoke an unintentional response, often pursed lips, or a sniff as though the colors emit a smell. Embarrassed, I lie, "The walls will be repainted soon. Don't worry."

I learn my office is to be shared. My office-mate is also a lecturer, one of the special lecturers like me, hired as part of the new model for fixed-term faculty. Each week, she travels far from home to teach here, so she sits in the office a lot, lacking anywhere else to go.

I decide I prefer the campus coffee shop for my office hours. And I buy a new desk for the spare bedroom in the bungalow to have a place to do my writing.

September 2007

They've repainted the hallways of the Bunker. The Bunker's windows don't open, so there's no fresh air. Near the mailboxes, I feel a bit lightheaded from the fumes. Dr. Cultural Studies stands next to me, fumbling with his mail, the same mail I've received, a tightly packed parcel of fliers, notices, and newsletters, each printed on a different shade of pastel paper.

We stand, our rainbows in our hands, and I say, "The paint smell sure is strong, don't you think?"

He says, without a sign of recognition in his eyes, "You should just be glad they painted." Then he turns and drops his rainbow in the trash.

I wonder if he talks to all faculty that way, or just the young ones, or just the women, or just the ones he doesn't know.

October 2007

I stand in the foyer of the Bunker, where Mr. Tall proposed to me, staring at the Board with its small white letters. My name still isn't there.

———

[one year passes]

———

The Freelance Academic

October 2008

My name does not belong on the Board, I'm told, because lecturers are itinerant, and because to purchase more small, white letters would cost the department too much money.

November 2008

I'm going to have a baby in June.

I hide in the bathroom when I feel sick, armed with a slick pack of lies: I sure gained the newly-wed fifteen, or, Avoid the sushi in the Union today. It's a little off.

December 2008

Faculty meeting. A new course scheduling policy. Each school year, all faculty must teach one semester of Monday, Wednesday, and Friday courses, no exceptions. Many groans emit.

Then, Dr. Twentieth Century says, her voice high and southern and sweet, "I don't see why we can't just have those lecturers teach three days a week. After all, they don't have to write. It's us researchers that should have the good schedules."

I remember some words my mother once said to me when I was in college. She said, "You grow up to be a doctor, do you hear me? Don't you grow up to be a nurse." At the time, I'd just declared an English major, so her words seemed a little strange.

Now I know what she meant. She's been married to a doctor for thirty years, running the practice for twenty. But to some, she'll always be just a doctor's wife.

I became a doctor. But I'm still a nurse. Except nurses get paid more and have better job security.

January 2009

My textbook proposal is accepted by a publisher. I sign my contract at a bistro with Mr. Tall, and he takes my picture with the pen in my hand.

The English Department lecturers form an advisory committee and ask for promotion procedures. We want a senior title, with senior pay, and five-year contracts. We form a listserv, start a newsletter with meeting minutes, and begin to plan.

Our push seems to be working.

Meanwhile, to make more money for when the baby comes, I take on an extra course teaching writing at a law school in another city, driving fifty miles each way to get there. The extra course seems like a sensible decision. I never thought I'd be a freeway flier to make ends meet, but I'm happy to have the work.

February 2009

My belly is starting to show, and I'm worried. In addition to English, I also majored in Women's Studies, so I can recognize my fear as an old one. My fear is one working women have felt for decades—that my boss will resent my pregnancy, the promised leave from work (right there in contractual black and white), and the distraction that a child brings.

I've made friends with another lecturer, Dr. Cool. She's been in the Bunker for sixteen years. I stop by her office one afternoon, nervous, needing someone to talk to. She invites me to sit in her office. It's hers alone, and it's bright, with pictures of her grown children on the walls. There are also pictures of Dr. Cool with famous writers she's worked with, like Joan Didion.

"Is your name on the Board?" I ask her.

"No," she says, "and it really makes me mad."

I tell her I'm pregnant. It seems she already knows. She says, "Honey, you should tell everybody. Then they sure as heck can't fire you."

I tell everyone.

I tell our new department chair. She reassures me that not only will I have a job when I get back from parental leave, but that she'll do all in her power to make it as good a job as she can. She tells me she is happy for me, and I believe her.

I sign a form that gives me a semester's paid leave in the fall, and at that moment, I'm really happy that I work in the Bunker.

March 2009

An announcement to all lecturers: Due to budget shortfalls, all lecturers will be placed on one-year contracts for the foreseeable future.

We are reassured, however, that the department—the tenured faculty—will do all it can to protect us.

April 2009

All faculty receive a golden-yellow announcement in the mail, asking for proposals for University-funded small research grants, given to the most promising research projects proposed by any faculty member.

In boldface, like a black eye, the form letter says, Adjunct professors are not eligible, nor are lecturers, instructors, or others of non-professorial rank.

I wonder, if the grants are truly based on merit, why they choose to exclude certain members of the faculty.

I think of high school, when I was a young player on the junior varsity volleyball team. During a preseason scrimmage against the varsity squad, we kicked their butts. Our ever-pragmatic coach simply admitted his error and traded squads, placing the J.V. players on varsity and benching his former starters. Ignoring their protests, he told them, You just need to play better, folks.

I'm starting to wonder about the meaning of merit in the Bunker.

May 2009

My son is born six weeks early.

His skinny, premature form lies in a plastic bin, wires tracking to machines that blip and flash. He eats through a tube. He's weighed every hour. He sleeps under heat lamps and the special UV lamps for jaundice. There are no windows in the nursery. I never know what time of day it is.

For one week he sleeps in that bin, and I forget the Bunker, the Board, the pink-and-yellow office, Dr. Cultural Studies and his disregard, Dr. Twentieth Century and her naïve insults. I think, *If my baby comes home to me safe, nothing else will ever matter again.*

I sit by his bin and grade final papers for my four writing courses. Grades are due in two days.

September 2009

Home with my son, enjoying generous parental leave, I feel like a hypocrite. Sure, no one dreams of growing up to be second-class. But, I tell myself, second-class academia is better than most jobs.

The state budget is getting ugly. Our new chair comes to a lecturers' meeting, where we're finalizing our proposal for the creation of a senior lecturer position. She says, "The budget has been deeply cut. It's not certain that you will all be rehired next year."

Suddenly, the promotion and retention proposal we've been debating, revising, and debating seems pointless.

After the Chair has left, one lecturer says, "We sure got put back in our places. The lecturers were getting uppity."

I go home and say to Mr. Tall, "We're playing *Survivor*. I'm going to lose."

The Freelance Academic

December 2009

In the last faculty meeting of the calendar year, the Senior Lecturer promotion proposal comes up for a vote. Due to budgetary constraints, the bits in the proposal about higher pay and longer contracts are excised. After six years of teaching, a lecturer can put in for a promotion to Senior Lecturer. At least the title will be better.

At the faculty meeting, I point out what appears to be a mistake in the paperwork. It says that all tenure-track faculty can vote on lecturers being promoted to senior lecturer. I think, a first-year assistant professor, who hasn't even passed third-year review, shouldn't be able to vote on a veteran such as Dr. Cool. That's absurd.

I raise my hand, and the chair recognizes me.

I say, "Shouldn't this say "tenured" faculty? Do we want assistant professors to vote on Senior Lecturers? Do we really think that all Assistant Professors are a higher rank than Senior Lecturers?"

The room, stuffed with sixty faculty members, is silent for a moment. Then, Dr. Linguist turns around to look at me, except she doesn't really look at me, just toward me. She says, "Yes, they are. I'm sorry, but that's just the way it is."

The chair nods. The motion passes.

I go to the departmental office. One of the administrators has been holding my son during the meeting with the sure hands of a grandmother. His small body is draped across her, his fist tucked into his mouth. I see my small boy lying on her chest, sleeping, and I shut the office door and cry.

January 2010

I come to the Bunker for the new semester, returning to teaching after a semester of leave. My textbook is in production. I did it all on my own, with no help from the Bunker. I'm proud of myself.

I walk into the Bunker's foyer, and the Board is down. Dr. Cool walks up to me and says, "Our names are going up. It's gonna happen today."

I say, "Is it silly that I'm so excited about this?"

In a world in which we always lose, we have finally won something. Standing next to Dr. Cool, I snap a picture of my name —well, Mr. Tall's name—on the new board, using my cell phone, and send it to Mr. Tall.

He writes back, "It's finally official."

I glance at Dr. Cool, her arms crossed, as she watches the letters adjust to accommodate us. And I wonder, *Is it, though? Can it ever be?*

PART I
Coming to Be a Freelance Academic

ONE

A Manifesto for the Freelance Academic

IN THE NEW, CORPORATE MODEL OF HIGHER EDUCATION, FACULTY OF all stripes, but most commonly those in contingent positions, find themselves pushed to the margins—of their departments, of their very institutions. If you're lucky enough to have a full-time contingent position, you often still feel like an outsider. Even if you have a tenure-track position, you can probably see that the system you are part of is unsustainable. After all, higher education's future is uncertain.

Welcome to the world of The Freelance Academic.

This book tells the story of my transition from a patchwork, contingent career in academia to a new career where I decided to approach my academic job as a freelancer—with all the benefits that come with that approach. After all, the universities I worked for already treated me like a freelancer; it was high time I acted like one. The decision to approach my academic career as a freelancer was incredibly freeing.

As faculty, we work in overstressed conditions with inadequate resources, many of us hoping that somehow—someday—the academic world will right itself again. But the academic world isn't going to right itself again. It's changing, and it's not going to change back. There aren't enough "real" jobs for the large number of graduate students finishing up their degrees because colleges are relying more and more on contingent labor rather than tenure-track labor with benefits and job security. To survive in this changing academic world in which institutions treat (most) academics as disposable, I realized that we, as academics, have to change, too.

My opening salvo for my new career was the following five-point Freelance Academic Manifesto, which I wrote when I left my full-time higher ed job. The purpose of the manifesto was to help contingent faculty (and all faculty who were feeling disempowered by their higher education employment) take some power back. I also wrote it because I needed a way to make decisions in the new academic paradigm. Because I felt like I'd lost my navigational points, I created new ones.

The five points of this manifesto apply to you whether you are contingent or tenure-track, whether you are new to the academy or on your way out. One thing is constant: the shame we feel for failing to meet the impossible standards that our jobs set for us, and the damage shame does to our mental health. The manifesto, then, is also a bulwark against the shame many faculty share and a shield for our mental health.

1. Get paid for your work.

When I contemplated the ending of my higher ed career, the first thing I told myself was this: Stop researching, writing, and editing for free. Get paid for your hard work. You deserve it.

After I'd edited yet another tenured colleague's scholarly article with no offer of reciprocation, I realized two things. First, I realized that I had a gift when it came to editing. Second, I realized that I could get paid for the work I was doing for free around my department.

Now, a lot of folks edit each other's work in academic departments as a part of their service work. Others do it to be collegial. Neither of those things applied to me. I didn't get service credit for the editing because scholarship wasn't part of my job description as a teaching-focused contingent faculty member. Scholarship was bonus work. And, after the third, fourth, or fifth time I edited someone's article without any reciprocation, I realized that my colleagues weren't being collegial. They were using me. One told me, "I'm not telling anyone else how good you are at this so that I can keep you all to myself." Her patronizing words made me feel small and demeaned, but I was unable to fight back because of my job position.

After I left, I started working as an editor, helping people place articles in top journals or books with top publishers. Sure, I still helped friends with their pieces, but only my real friends, and I figured out who they were. I didn't let myself be used out of some misplaced hope that I would be accepted into the cool club someday. After I started working as a professional editor, the professors I helped knew that they need editorial assistance, and many of their institutions gave them professional development funds to hire editors, so I met that need (as do other professional editors like I was).

I know getting started as a paid freelancer can be intimidating. Mulling over the plusses and minuses of working for yourself can help you make better decisions, as Kelly J. Baker noted in her 2014 column on shifting her career to freelance writing ("To Write or Not to Write").[1] In fact, I recommend that you read everything you can about how to start making money for the hard work you do. Gathering information about money, running a business, and what it actually takes to turn your skills into rent and food is a crucial step you must take.

While you are taking good advice, please, do not listen to people who tell you flat out that you can't do it. There are a lot of naysayers out there. I don't know what their problem is. Just ignore them. I know it's hard, especially after being demeaned and shamed for so long in higher education. When your mental health has been battered, it can be hard to believe in yourself.

The heart of the getting-paid point is this simple fact: You are worth more than your institution pays you. When you are contingent faculty, earning a few hundred bucks for writing a short magazine article in your area of expertise means groceries for your family for the month. Instead of taking on unpaid work in your department to catch someone's eye (maybe), earn some cash writing for a national audience and catch everyone's eye. Or spend some time working on a website for yourself to establish your national presence as an expert.

Speaking of that extra departmental labor: Getting paid also means when your institution asks you to take on extra work, you ask for extra money. When someone not in your institution asks you to do labor in your area of expertise, bill them, politely.

You have a living to make.

There is one exception to the get-paid rule: Love. If you truly love something, you can do it for free. But never forget that the "love" of higher ed has long been used to keep contingent faculty poor.[2] Love can trick us into doing things for free when we should be getting paid. Whatever you do, don't get snookered by the "love" thing. We contingent faculty have been told for so long that money sullies the life of the mind. I call malarkey. As author and former academic Sarah Kendzior wrote in 2013, "Should academics ever write for free? Maybe. Should academics write for free for a publisher that can afford to pay them? Never."[3]

My theory about writing for free is this: There are a lot of great magazines out there that editors run for nothing. The staff don't make money, the writers don't make money—the entire enterprise is a labor of love. Sometimes, the magazine even loses money. *What's the point?* you might ask. The point is to publish stories that will make the world a better place. Early in my freelance academic career, I used to write for magazines like that a lot. But if a magazine can afford to pay and it doesn't? That's exploitation, plain and simple. If it can afford to pay well, and pays poorly? Same. Mostly, you should never be shy about talking about money, and a publication shouldn't be shy about it either. It can be hard to ignore the shame you might feel about money-talk, especially because years in higher education teaches us that talking about money is uncouth. But shame wears down our mental resources just as avoiding money-talk wears down our financial resources.

2. Live in a place you love with the people you love.

Here's when love should matter to your decision matrix.

Academia teaches you to move away from the people and places you love in order to be successful. Academia shames us into believing we have to be willing to move anywhere to find any job, otherwise we aren't dedicated enough.

When I was on the job market fresh out of graduate school, I turned down fancier jobs all over the country for my first contingent job. But I took that contingent job in order to be able to stay with my husband, to stay in a really nice place to live, and also to stay where both my and my husband's parents live. I traded the tenure track for my humanity. Unintentionally, way back then, I followed point number two on my manifesto. I'm so glad that I did. If I hadn't, I'd likely be where I am today—out of academia—but without the family I love around me.

The problem I faced out of graduate school wasn't one of choosing my family over my career. The problem is that academia, as a career, has become so broken that we have to make this choice in the first place.

Academia shames us into making a choice between our humanity and our careers. Living away from the people we love is the opposite of living as a human being. It is bad for us, physically and mentally. If you have the choice, live with your family in a place where you enjoy living. Don't let anyone tell you that you are copping out by choosing your happiness over your academic credentials.

In a similar vein, if you want to have children, have children—create new, small people to love. And if you don't want to, don't.

And if you can't, remember that you don't have to explain your private business.[4]

3. When you find yourself being lured back to your department for a temporary gig, remember: They're never going to let you in the club.

Stop hoping that the department where you are contingent is suddenly going to recognize that you are awesome (despite the fact that you are, indeed, awesome). They're not going to suddenly offer you a tenure-track job. No matter how awesome you are, it just won't happen. So long as you hold out a glimmer of hope that it will, your department will hold all the power.

And so long as they hold the power, you will keep taking on more free work, hoping that someone will tap you with a magic wand and make you a special fairy, too. It's never going to happen. Grieve. Accept. Move on.

Now, step back and embrace the freelance academic mindset. Now you hold the power. You no longer have only one path to success—the path through traditional academic tracks. Now you have a universe of paths.

4. Stop applying to academic jobs.

The job market is too expensive—temporally, financially, and emotionally. The chances of the perfect job being right around the corner are slim to none. The longer you're off the market working as contingent faculty, the worse your application appears because departments prefer new Ph.D.s over ones with experience.

This is yet another way that academia is completely backwards. I had a very hard time explaining this hiring paradox to my highly practical mother. "You mean your experience works against you? That's preposterous!"

Yes, it's preposterous. Fortunately, it doesn't matter. You're a freelance academic now. So use the time and money you will save by not applying for jobs to start freelancing. For example, if you want to write, take a course on how to pitch ideas to writer's markets that pay, either through online courses or by hiring a successful freelancer friend to teach you. The course I took paid for itself within a week after I sold a story that I had workshopped during the course.

I know it's hard to let go of the dream of landing the perfect academic job. You think, Just one more round of applications, and I'll be in. You won't be in. I'm so sorry. You sound like someone who buys lottery tickets. Stop buying lottery tickets. They're bad for your wallet and your soul.

5. Remember that you are not alone.

Turning your academic knowledge and skills into cash is, itself, a skill. But there are people out there who can help you. Hire an academic career coach, one who specializes in helping people transition out of the academy entirely, if that's what you want to do. Find support locally and on social media, building a group of people who believe in you. There will, of course, be jerks—the naysayers who will tell you that what you want to do is too hard or even impossible. Oh, jeez, please do ignore them.

After I wrote this manifesto, I could finally navigate my way out of higher ed. Before I could change my career, I had to change my belief system. The manifesto gave me the strength to do so.

Is "freelance academic" the right term?

I once received an email from a reader of an essay who told me that, while she found my ideas about my career transition to be generally strong, she did not like the term "freelance academic" at all. Oddly enough, she had no problem with the "academic" part but rather with "freelance." I know that the reader meant well. Generally, her tone was supportive. But she spent a paragraph explaining how the term "freelance" connotes "inferiority" and "lack of expertise." It's a word a person uses, she told me, because they couldn't find a full-time job.

In her words I could see the shame that I frequently find when I talk to people who have struggled in higher education. They don't want to let go of the status they believe higher education confers. The word "inferiority" stuck out to me, as did "lack of expertise." Then there was the notion of "full-time." Contingent faculty are frequently made to feel that we're *inferior*, that if we had *greater expertise*, then we could get that *full-time* tenure-track job. Right? (Wrong. There just aren't any tenure-track jobs.[5])

The letter-writer recommended a different term: "Independent scholar." I've seen others use that phrase often enough, but it's not synonymous with "freelance academic." Independent scholar does not, at all, describe the work that I do. For example, I do not write scholarship anymore. Instead, I write for money. Unless you have a tenure-track position that pays you a salary because of your scholarship, the pay for publishing journal articles is nil. Thus, while "independent scholar" may describe very well what others do, it does not describe what freelance academics do.

But what about the second term in my chosen title, "academic"? In debates over labels like "alternative academic" or "post-academic," I've heard other people express dislike of the use of "academic." Some of the arguments seem to suggest that when a person clings to the "academic" label, they are clinging to academia itself.

So I went to the dictionary. Oxford defines the adjective "academic," firstly, in this fashion: "of or relating to education and scholarship." I've already decided that scholarship, as such, is no longer for me.

But there's that other word—"education." I still do a lot with education. For example, I cover a higher education beat in my freelance journalism (for money). I give paid talks that educate people about my areas of expertise, which include mental health and higher education. For a long while, I wrote textbooks to help people learn, and I write new editions when needed. I worked as a developmental editor to help writers finish their manuscripts and get them out to publishers—educating my clients about writing.

I'm immersed in education, and my academic training has allowed me to do this work. It seems to me, then, that "freelance academic" is just the right term.

TWO

What Does It Mean to Be a Freelance Academic?

In May of 2014, I took a one-year, unpaid leave of absence from my contingent academic job. The year prior, I earned a promotion to a senior position with relative job security and fairly good pay, considering that I would never have tenure. But when my department head called me to give me the happy news, I thanked him quickly, hung up the phone, and cried. Being promoted brought my life into focus: I'd been working eighty-hour weeks to achieve a goal I wanted nothing to do with. I hated my job.

I'd gone from loving my work to feeling trapped, overworked, and exploited. My mental health was tanked. I was in full burnout; I just didn't realize it. I just knew something had to change. I did good work—good enough that when I requested a year's leave after being promoted, they gave it to me. Unpaid, of course, and I'd have to cover all of my expenses, too, like health insurance, because I was contingent. While my tenure-track colleagues got their post-tenure sabbaticals fully funded by the school, I paid for mine out of pocket. But I was grateful they gave me the leave. Because now I had a year to figure out whether I wanted to go back at all.

I had a year to figure out if I could make it as a freelancer.

Here's what I did right away, even before I formally left for my leave. As soon as my request was granted—early in the spring semester—I started making some changes.

I changed my website's design from one that was basically an online C.V. for a faculty member to one that was an online portfolio about me.

I gave the website a title: *The Freelance Academic*. I'd been toying with that title for a while. I bought the URL (freelanceacademic.com) and redirected it toward my website (which was katieroseguestpryal.com)

I started blogging a lot more, and I started blogging about things important to me: I wrote about the state of higher education, sexual assault law, mental health and neurodiversity, and politics. I shared my point of view. On the blog, I started establishing my areas of expertise.

These changes might not sound like much, but for a contingent faculty member, they were a big deal because they were risky.

One important note: before I left higher education, I had some skills in web design. Once I decided to take my hiatus, I learned more. So when I say that I redesigned my website, I mean that I did it myself. And once I realized that I would be leaving academia for good, I decided to teach myself even more about website design, coding, and hosting. I studied tutorials online to add to what I already knew. Everything I studied was free. I recommend learning how to design your own website so that you can maintain a professional web presence. If you can learn even more and offer website design as a freelance skill, even better.

What all of these changes amounted to was this: I dumped my online academic identity and claimed one as a freelancer—even while very much maintaining my contingent post at a university. On the blog, I stepped outside of the boundaries of acceptable academic discourse. I engaged in what one of my doctoral advisors had once called "fist-waving" while frowning at an article I'd written. It wasn't a compliment. Ever since then, I'd felt hamstrung by the need to come across as measured and distant from the topics I examined in my academic writing.

But no longer. Now that I had distance from academia, I could be a better writer, one with voice and fire.

It's easy to look back on this time of transition, now, years later, and see my trajectory out of academia as smooth and simple. But it wasn't. The transition was filled with uncertainty, both career-wise and money-wise. One of the reasons I wanted to write this book is to document that uncertainty, to leave breadcrumbs for others to follow. I wanted to show exactly what I did (to the best of my memory), so that others can see that, although it isn't easy, starting your own career after higher ed can be done.

One of the many problems with being inside of academia is that you cannot see the proverbial forest for the trees. As higher education critic Rebecca Schuman has accurately put it, academia suffers from a "cult mentality" that is hard to see until you step away from it.[1] Schuman describes how the cult works: doctoral programs "isolate graduate students from the outside world," then "break the students down" by trashing their intellectual labor. Next, "shortly before they defend their dissertations, [graduate programs] call them 'brilliant' and fill their heads with dreams of R1 glory," that is, of high-end academic jobs. They "make sure they know there is no other noble path outside the Life of the Mind." On the job market, students and recent grads bust their asses doing everything expected of them "on the off chance that someone, somewhere might hire us." But if they want to critique the system, they use a pseudonym, "which ties into the final way in which academe resembles a cult: abject terror of being shunned."

The point is, most, if not all, graduate students are taught by their professors to view the academy as the only viable profession for them. I was taught the same. In the newsletter from my department, they print updates about the department's graduates, but they only send updates if you have landed a tenure-track job. If you have chosen a profession outside the academy, they don't want to share it. We are their ugly secrets. Our former departments signal to us in myriad ways that we should feel ashamed of failing after working for years to achieve the elite status of a doctoral degree holder.

This shaming does a number on a person's mental health. Research shows that failure after high-level training can cause depression. For example, a psychological study of elite athletes shows that failure to achieve a goal causes depression in 80% of cases. This type of response is called "failure-based depression."[2]

In order to escape feelings of failure and shame, I needed to make some changes to my mindset and to my identity. So I professionalized myself as a freelance academic, even though I didn't have a new profession yet. They tell you to "fake it till you make it," so I started faking it, right away.

As I turned in my final set of grades and stepped away from my contingent teaching job, I discovered something important.

When you're a contingent academic, you are bifurcated into two professional beings. Half of you is the being the university insists you become. But then there is the remainder of you, what's left, the parts that the university doesn't want. Often, those parts are the very best of you. What happens to the researcher, if you are in a teaching position that doesn't value or support research? The innovator? The leader? All of those skills and gifts that the institution doesn't want—worse, wishes you didn't have?

What do you do with the leftovers? Squelch them down? Let them wither?

This bifurcation played out for me like this: There was the Katie who worked at my contingent teaching job, working fifty to sixty hours per week course planning, curriculum designing, lesson writing, student conferencing, and grading. I worked and worked and worked, hoping that I wouldn't actually feel bifurcated at all. I hoped I could fool myself.

It didn't work.

So then there was the Katie who worked on the side seeking to complete the teaching/research intellectual circle. There was no space in my contingent job description for the research and writing, unlike for my tenure-track counterparts. So I squeezed in writing on the side, in the evenings, on the weekends. I wrote novels (two), poetry, short stories (even published some), articles (I published so many! No one cared), conference presentations, and textbooks (three). My workweek added up to eighty to a hundred hours a week. It was, in a word, unsustainable. I burned out.

I also felt like I had a split personality. Like I worked three jobs. Like I was a terrible mother. Enter the surprise personal crisis and my request for leave. And that was that.

To be a freelance academic is to recognize this bifurcation that we contingent faculty face, and then to try to mend it. Yes, I worked for a university as a contingent professor. But I also wrote and researched. I realized that I didn't have to let any part of me be squelched or allowed to wither. When we wither, our mental health suffers.

But I couldn't keep working hundred-hour weeks, either. That wasn't good for my health or the health of my family. But in order to stop, my goals had to shift. Indeed, the biggest change required to become a freelance academic is to recognize that, in the words of a dear friend from grad school, *They're never going to let you in the club.*

THREE

On Not Writing

JOB INSECURITY, ANXIETY, AND ENTERING PUBLIC LIFE

IN MARCH OF 2014, WHEN I ASKED FOR A ONE-YEAR LEAVE OF absence from my contingent faculty job starting that May, the entire spring semester I struggled with my identity. I knew I needed to change things about my career, sure, but I also needed to change some things about myself.

I'd spent the entire school year working toward a promotion—from "assistant" contingent faculty to "associate" contingent faculty. I put together a full promotion book. I published research articles and gave talks at conferences, even though, as contingent faculty, my research didn't really count toward my promotion, not like it did for tenure-track faculty. But I also knew that the people who voted on my promotion were all tenure-track faculty, and they valued research as much or more than they valued teaching. I needed to make myself legible to them.

I taught my classes, crafting new curriculum along the way. I taught so well that my supervisor asked me to train the newly hired faculty (not that I got any extra money for that extra work). I was an expert. I was excellent. Surely, that would be enough.

I worked so hard, in fact, that I felt like I was finally earning my place on the faculty. I ignored, actively, the signals that told me otherwise. My pay was one-half to one-third what the tenure-track faculty earned. I didn't have their other benefits, such as research assistants or research funding or even mentorship. And I didn't have job security. In short, I didn't have so many of the things that tenure-track faculty took for granted.

I told myself that, if I could just get promoted, I could ask for those things, and the department would give them to me. How could they not? I would have earned them.

When, in early December, the faculty voted to promote me, I felt like I had achieved something. Finally. But moments after, I realized that I'd been working toward an empty goal.

Promotion to what?

Who dreams of being promoted to yet another contingent job?

In fact, I didn't even get a pay raise. I got a new title, a renewed contract, and nothing else. Even worse, when I asked for a raise, I got a very ugly email from the head of my division telling me that I was overstepping, and it firmly put me back in my place.

After working toward that one goal for so long, I needed to recalibrate. But I didn't know how.

Like most writers, I wanted to write about my experiences to help make sense of them. But writing about my experiences as contingent faculty presented its own challenges, especially because I was still employed by a university. I didn't feel like I had the freedom to write about the politics of higher education while I was still mired in them because I was afraid that I'd get fired. Retribution for contingent faculty who speak publicly is a real risk.[1]

How do you critique a system when you rely on that system to survive? All I wanted to write about was the higher education system that I'd been a part of for over a decade. My eyes were opening, and I wanted to share my discoveries. But I couldn't. I was stymied.

The spring of my last semester teaching, my colleague and friend Ariane and I were having a heart-to-heart over coffee in order to avoid grading papers.

She said, "I want to spend the summer writing a fun book, not academic research." A fun book to her meant a hardboiled mystery like something P.D. James would write. (James was her favorite author.) Ever since Ariane was a kid, she only ever wanted to be a writer.

In response, I immediately said "me too"—but this wouldn't be surprising information about me, since I majored in English and have a master's in creative writing. Ariane, for her part, majored in biology. At the time of this conversation, of course, we were both first-year writing professors off the tenure-track.

We faced one of the challenges that contingent faculty always face: If you have the luxury to have time to write, do you write scholarship with the hope of forwarding your academic career, or do you write something you might find more fun, and hope to publish it another way?

Of course, all of this writing presupposed that the stacks of papers got graded.

The bigger question is this: since contingent faculty are no less driven or intelligent or educated than our tenure-track colleagues, what do we do with the remainder that is left over after we do the work required of us for our contingent jobs? What do we do with the remainder that our employers do not want from us, all that creative energy that they do not even want to know we have? Do we hope that our work will one day get us tenure-track recognition?

Or do we do something else?

At the time of this conversation with Ariane, I'd been writing a lot, working hard to finish open projects. Almost all of my works-in-progress were scholarly articles or conference presentations. Yet I was in a job that did not pay me for my research. Indeed, some colleagues (and I use that term loosely) grumbled that my research distracted me from my teaching, and they preferred that faculty in contingent positions like mine didn't do research at all.

I realized, at that moment, that I didn't have a vision for the future of my writing at all. I had a mounting stack of unpublished book manuscripts (with no time to market them to publishers) and conference papers that would never be articles (because more and more I didn't see the point in rewriting them for journals). I wasn't even writing on my blog—it had been a year since my previous blog post.

So I found myself back to where both my colleague and I began our conversation: we were writers. In particular, writers who taught first-year writing and who didn't have a lot of spare time to write for ourselves.

Now that I had a premise to start from, I finished the stack of papers and tried to create a vision for what would come next.

A few days later, I gave more thought to why I hadn't been writing on what is, essentially, my professional blog.

I finally landed on the very specific reason: fear.

Every time I sat down to give thoughtful written analysis of the topic that had been at the front of my mind, I self-censored out of fear. I was afraid I would lose my job if I wrote about the inequities and other problems in higher education. I have an anxiety disorder, but you don't need to have anxiety to be afraid for your job.

Fear was always with me when I would sit down to write about a topic that had been at the front of my mind, such as critiques of higher education or teaching. Although I'd already written on these topics for scholarly journals, I had not written on these topics in the far more personal forum of a blog.

I was afraid to write about how working in higher ed affected me, personally. How life off of the tenure track had changed my life, my career, and my image of myself. I didn't know how to write these critiques from a position as myself, Katie, rather than from a position as a scholar, without putting my job on the line. So I didn't write at all.

I didn't know how to get around this fear that was hampering my ability to write, so I went on social media and asked for advice: "How do you blog about work inequities without losing your job?"

The Freelance Academic

I got some great responses. One came from digital pedagogy expert and higher education critic Lee Skallerup Bessette who wrote a blog for *Inside Higher Education*. Because of the public nature of her blog, her response to me was exceptionally funny: "Put your blog on the most visible platform you can—that way no one at your [institution] will notice."[2] Then she followed up: "Seriously. Not one person at my [university] reads my blog."

Apparently, the first step to breaking through the anxiety-driven writer's block I was experiencing was to realize that I was a grain of sand in the ocean of words on the Internet. Easy enough.

Bessette followed up with even more substantive advice, advice that later responses to my question seemed to follow: "Be honest and always link [your writing] to the larger trends and structural issues."

Okay, I thought. That makes sense. Linking any critique to larger trends makes a critique more substantive, less like a hatchet job and more like journalism (or even, gasp, scholarship). And it follows that this substantive critique would hopefully be protected by something like academic freedom (if academic freedom actually protected the jobs of contingent faculty). Plus, a substantive critique must be less likely to raise hackles, right? I didn't realize it at the time, but by clinging to writing that resembled scholarship, I was assuaging my anxiety. I eventually let go of that.

Bessette's first bit of advice seems to be her most important: "Be honest." Critiques of higher education must be grounded in honest, clear-eyed observations of the inequities that surround us every day in the academic workplace. These are the observations that no one wants to talk about in faculty meetings or on committees (if one is allowed to go to faculty meetings or join committees). Thus, one person's "hatchet job" might be another person's "clear-eyed observation"—especially when the person feeling the hatchet has tenure and the person making the observation is contingent.

Some of the most important evidence that supports critiques of higher education is the anecdotal experience of contingent faculty; our honesty is valuable. Setting aside my anxiety, and armed with this mindset, I started writing.

Then, a few days later, even more clarity struck from the outside. Nicholas Kristof bemoaned in his *New York Times* column how academics don't participate as public intellectuals anymore.[3] Kristof lamented the retreat by academics from public life. He wrote: "There are plenty of exceptions, of course…But, overall, there are, I think, fewer public intellectuals on American university campuses today than a generation ago." Kristof doesn't give a source for this change from then to now, just his gut. The reason for this change, though? Snobbery: "A basic challenge is that Ph.D. programs have fostered a culture that glorifies arcane unintelligibility while disdaining impact and audience. This culture of exclusivity is then transmitted to the next generation through the publish-or-perish tenure process. Rebels are too often crushed or driven away." Anyways, Kristof was basically saying that academia, due to its snobbish culture, is failing the world, and the world is worse off for it.

Suppose there are fewer public intellectuals on college campuses these days than there were a generation ago. Kristof couldn't imagine that something else might be the cause for the change, something beyond a culture of exclusivity. Something material, measurable. Something like the adjunctification of the professoriate that has taken place over the precise period of time that he points to.

Fortunately, political science professor Corey Robin handled this very issue in a response to Kristoff, pointing out how the vast majority of professors do not participate in public life for one simple reason: they can't.[4] Indeed, Robin touched on the particular reasons why I, personally, had not participated in public life when I was contingent faculty, reasons that Kristof completely overlooks in his piece. Robin writes, "Writers and academics who fret over the fate of public intellectuals may think they are debating vital questions of the culture. But their discussions are myopically focused on the writing habits of a rapidly disappearing elite." The elite that Robin refers to? The tenured professor.

If faculty are participating in public life less and less, that's because there are fewer and fewer tenured professors. Robin writes, "The vast majority of potential public intellectuals do not belong to the academic 1 percent [that is, tenured faculty]. They are not forsaking the snappy op-ed for the arcane article. They are not navigating the shoals of publish or perish. They're grading." Contingent faculty don't have the time or the job security to participate in public life. They're teaching four or five sections across multiple campuses to keep food on the table.

Robin's piece addressed not only how overworked contingent faculty are, but also the precariousness of their jobs. This lack of job security might lead academic intellectuals with otherwise interesting public ideas to keep such ideas to themselves: "Nearly three-quarters of all instructional staff at colleges and universities today are not on the tenure track. They're insecure, contingent workers, an army of cheap and casual labor that make the universities go. While young writers can afford to do the kind of intellectual journalism we see at the little magazines, older adjuncts teaching five classes can't." Not only do they lack the time, but they also can't risk their jobs by taking a public stand that might cause their institutions to fire them. Institutions can fire contingent faculty if they don't like what the contingent faculty say, and institutions have done so.

One of the most pressing issues in higher education today is the very statistic that Robin mentions above: nearly three-quarters of higher education faculty are contingent. That means that many of those best situated to write about higher education are those who are most afraid of losing their jobs in higher education.

For many years, I was an "older adjunct," one with two children and a mortgage. I spent my first four years after graduate school terrified that I would lose my contingent job, playing a game of *Survivor* initiated by a department chair who told us that each year some of us wouldn't be rehired, that each spring she would review our teaching evaluations and only keep the best. My anxiety was through the roof. Chronic stress kept me up at night and made me irritable at home. It was a horrible way to live when I had a family depending on me.

One eye-opening moment occurred in the hospital. I had a premature baby, and a young resident doctor in the Neonatal Intensive Care Unit told me that my baby might have come prematurely because I managed my stress poorly while pregnant —as though I had some kind of choice given my work conditions.

Corey Robin's column asked an important question: Given our precariousness and our heavy workloads, what can the world ask of contingent intellectuals?

My answer is, so long as we rely on our departments for our entire livelihoods, not much. For me, something had to change. And that change became The Freelance Academic.

FOUR

On Writing

MAKING YOUR WRITING MATTER

IN MAY OF 2014, I HIT AT A CRITICAL MOMENT IN MY ACADEMIC career. After eleven years teaching as contingent faculty, all the while searching for a tenure-track job, I decided to quit searching. I gave up seeking something that I was never going to get and wasn't sure I wanted anyway.

Here's what I did instead: I wrote an early draft of the "Freelance Academic Manifesto" on my blog, and I decided I had better ways to spend my time and money than on the academic job search.

It wasn't easy, but I walked away—not only from the job search, but eventually from full-time academia altogether.

When I gave up the job search, other things in my life changed as well. Essential to being on a perpetual academic job search is the requirement to publish as many articles as one can in academic journals and edited collections. The job search also requires presenting at as many prestigious professional conferences as possible. The last few years before I quit the job search, I ran myself into the ground trying to make my C.V. as impressive as possible, hoping to land a tenure-track job.

While publishing all of those words and traveling to give all of those presentations, I was also missing milestones: my older kid lost his first tooth while I was off giving a talk at a conference. I got to chat with him about it on FaceTime.

Guess what: It wasn't the same.

To use higher education writer Rebecca Schuman's term, I was performing "adjunct heroics" (not a term of praise) hoping that my tenured colleagues would grant me membership in the tenure-track club.[1] But finally, after eleven years, I figured out that that was never going to happen. How did I figure it out? I asked the head of my division, and he said that I would never be considered for a tenure-track job. Ever. His words were like a punch in the face, but they were also incredibly freeing.

I stopped writing academic articles. But I did not stop writing.

One afternoon, I received an email from a reporter at a popular magazine, asking to interview me about a current event: the forthcoming publication of novelist Harper Lee's book, *Go Set a Watchman*, and the apparent downfall of Atticus Finch as an American hero. I agreed to the interview. Before the reporter could begin the interview, I asked her a question: "How did you find me?"

I figured she saw something I wrote on social media or my blog.

No, she said. She'd found me through my research.

Many years prior, I published an article on *To Kill a Mockingbird* that took a controversial, critical stance on Atticus Finch. Based on that research article, the reporter believed I would be a good expert to interview about the new controversy surrounding the much-beloved character.

The next day, another reporter from another popular magazine called to interview me about the same topic. I gave another interview. Part of me found the entire situation hilarious, because my scholarship on the subject was published in such a minor venue and so very long ago. But the reporters were not wrong—I was indeed a good source. I did know what I was talking about, after I'd reread my own article to prepare for the interview.

How did they find my research, though? And what, exactly,

made me a good source? I did a few things right, things that anyone can and should do, especially any contingent faculty looking to transition to a life as a freelance academic.

First, I made my research publicly available by posting it on my own website and on open-access repositories that are indexed in search engines. My repository of choice is the Social Science Research Network, or SSRN. By posting my research online and ensuring that it was indexed, I'd made my research easy to find and had broken down the paywalls that kept my work from the general public.

Second, I did something else equally important, and far more frightening. I agreed to the interviews in the first place. I agreed, even though I was nervous and afraid of sounding stupid. I was also afraid of being thought an imposter. After all, I was never a "real professor," and I was not faculty at all anymore—right? If you have anxiety like I do, setting aside this fear might be the hardest part of all. But you can do it.

After a long conversation with myself after which I finally just told my inner critic to shut up, I answered the questions with all of the fake confidence I could muster. It wasn't long into the interview before the fake confidence turned into real confidence. And it wasn't long after that that I became the expert the reporters believed me to be.

I truly was the public intellectual speaking about one of the masterpieces of American literature.

Who, me? Yes, me. Frankly, it was weird. But at the same time, it was the most natural thing in the world. After all, why not me? I did the work. Why not me, indeed? Why not you?

I'm telling this story because I want to encourage you to put yourself in a position to engage publicly with your research. Freelance academics are perfectly aligned with the work of public engagement—but too often we worry that we aren't. We feel like imposter academics.

After all, if we were real academics, we'd have tenure, right?

That is so not true.

One of the problems that contingent faculty face is the double-bind of academic publishing: if we want to advance our academic careers, we must publish jargon-filled research in paywalled journals—work that we're usually not paid for because our jobs are teaching-track rather than research-track. Academics who bet on the insular system of higher education find themselves stranded when that system fails them, as it does most of us.

On the other hand, if we want to hedge our bets, to do work as freelance academics writing for the public in popular magazines, writing textbooks, or performing other non-insular tasks, then we run the risk of appearing non-academic, non-serious.

That's the double bind: (1) Make yourself attractive to a field where you are unlikely to find work by publishing articles that are hard to locate, read, and understand. Or: (2) Make yourself attractive to fields outside of academia by publishing your work in an accessible fashion (easy to locate and easy to read)—but risk making yourself seem non-academic as a result. Appeasing the academy means alienating alternatives.

Author and former academic Sarah Kendzior points out how this double bind works in practice: "To 'count' is to preserve your professional viability by shoring up disciplinary norms. In most fields, it means to publish behind a paywall, removed from the public eye—and from broader influence and relevance. To 'count' is to conform."[2] Kendzior laments the rule of academic publishing that requires hiding your work in order give it value. Instead, she says, "What 'counts' should be producing work of lasting intellectual value instead of market ephemerality. What 'counts' should be the quality of the research and writing, not the professional advantages you gain from producing it." Furthermore, as Kendzior points out, accessibility on both the readability front and actually getting-your-hands-on-it front are equally important. So much academic writing is hidden behind publication paywalls, which require the purchase of an article or membership to a university library. Then, when a reader finally can download an article, the knowledge it contains is hidden behind field-specific jargon, much of which is unnecessary for the making of meaning.

This lack of accessibility means that often no one outside of a narrow field can put to use the important ideas that many, if not most, scholars are developing today. And yet, embracing this inaccessibility is required in order for your academic colleagues and potential employers to take you seriously as a scholar.

There are a few steps that you can take to make your path to public engagement easier while still maintaining your professional credentials. And if you have accepted that a unicorn of a tenure-track job is never going to come your way, all the better—because your path to public engagement just got a whole lot easier. You don't have to worry about what scholarly colleagues think. You only have to worry about what you think. That's what I did, and it was incredibly freeing.

After I gave up on finding a tenure-track job, I made sure that my scholarly writing was out there, just as it is, available on a public repository and on my website. And speaking of a website, I created an Internet presence for myself so people could have a sense of who I am as a thinker and writer—as a freelance academic. And then, I took that final step and started writing my ideas for popular audiences. I did so by learning to pitch popular articles in my areas of expertise, to write them, and, when appropriate, to get paid for them. Here is how you can get started doing the same.

Step 1. Get Your Research Out There, Just as It Is.

If you have publications—articles, book chapters, books—they are likely not easily accessible on the Internet. You can change that. You can get them off your bookshelf and break down the paywalls. You can make it easy for readers to find your scholarship. Work with open-source repositories that are indexed in search engines. If you are with an institution, many have their own repositories. But I recommend a repository that allows you to maintain your independence from an institution, such as SSRN—the Social Science Research Network. It's free to use with good instructions for how to upload your research, and you don't need to be affiliated with an institution to have an account. It is well-indexed in search engines, which means that your work is easy to find.

Once you create an account, you can start uploading PDFs of your articles, chapters, and even select chapters from books you have written. Warning: Some uptight academic publishers get really freaked out when you put a PDF of your own article up on SSRN or other repositories because they hold the copyright to that particular printing of the article. They will send you angry emails demanding that you take it down. They'll email SSRN, too, and force that site to take it down.

This behavior is very annoying, especially since the work belongs to you, right? Don't worry. There are very legal workarounds. You have the right to make your work publicly available in two ways, even when your work is published by uptight companies.

First, you can upload the PDF of the actual journal article to your own website along with some language the publishers require you to use about it being an "author posting." So long as you are posting it to your own website, and not a repository, you can post the original PDF as much as you'd like. The problem, though, is that your own website is not well indexed in search engines.

Second, you have a right to post on public repositories a PDF of your own creation. Such a PDF is called an "author's version" of an article—say, a PDF of the final Word doc that you submitted for publication. That work will be indexed in search engines. Then, in the abstract in the repository, and on the PDF itself, you can note that the final PDF is available on your website.

By the time you, dear reader, come across this book, SSRN might be long gone in our rapidly changing technological landscape. But something else will have taken its place.

Whichever repository you choose, know that you have the right to share your work with the world, and you don't have to rely on institutional access to do it.

Step 2. Create an Internet Presence.

If you want to be a freelance academic, then you need a website. Here are some suggestions. Buy a web address that is your name. Why your name? Your name is forever whereas your "brand" might change. You can buy additional web addresses that are related to your brand (for instance, I also own "freelanceacademic.com"), and then you point them to your main website.

When you are building your website, start simply. Put your education and experience on an "About Me" page—think of it as your online C.V. or résumé. But put your publications on a separate webpage so that they're easy to skim: a "My Publications" page. Then, on the page with your publications, link your publications to whatever repository you use. You can also upload your author copies of your publications right there on your website, making it as easy as possible for readers to find your work.

After you start feeling confident about your website, try adding a blog. Blogs are a great way to test out ideas and share them. Blog posts can be short, and you can turn off comments so that you don't have to deal with trolls. You can automatically share your blog posts on social media—that's a function available through most blogging hosts. I highly recommend a blog. Indeed, after those Harper Lee interviews, I promptly wrote a blog post about them, adding more ideas that I couldn't share in the interviews, and adding my point of view as a writer, not just as an interview subject.

Speaking of social media: it is a great way to network, share your writing, and make connections. Platforms ebb and flow (as we saw with the demise of Twitter), but new ones grow to take their place (as LinkedIn did, surprisingly, after Twitter fell). If you're intimidated by social media, find a friend who is not and sit next to them for an afternoon until you get the hang of it. Social media is worth using for the community you can build, and it is essential to creating your Internet presence.

Step 3. Share Your Ideas—Widely

Once you've put your research online and created an Internet presence, it's time to take the next step: rewrite your research into popular articles. (Later in this book, I provide detailed information about how to write for the public.)

Whether your degree is in a STEM field or the humanities, you can find popular media outlets ready to pay you money (though not necessarily a lot of it) to write about your area of expertise. You'll need to spend some time figuring out which sites are interested in which genres. And you'll have to learn how to pitch articles and how to write the sort of pieces the venues want. You might not be able to make a living selling these pieces (after all, they pay bagels), but you can engage.

Remember, learning to be a freelance writer is hard. You have to learn a wide variety of new skills. I learned them by taking an online course. Back in 2014, the course cost $200; they're probably more expensive now, but you shouldn't pay much more than that. I earned it back one week after finishing the course when I sold one of the stories I developed during the course, and I'm still friends with the person who taught it. Most importantly, I learned so much about the day-to-day lives of freelance writers: how much money we make, how to pay taxes, how to invoice, and how to approach editors. I learned when to write for free (sometimes if for a good cause and the magazine has no money), and when not to write for free (when you simply can't afford to, or when they can afford to pay you).

It's worth learning how to do it right. Get started by reading the magazines you want to write for. Learn who the editors are by reading their work. And then, take the leap. Start pitching articles in your area of expertise that are "pegged" (tied) to current events. Turn your discerning academic eye outward. Those coffee-shop conversations about what's wrong with the world? Write them down.

And then sell them.

Before you know it, you will have begun engaging with both your area of academic expertise and with the world around you in new ways. It will be thrilling and a little bit scary, but you will continue to learn and grow, too. You will make mistakes. Ugh, so many mistakes. But you will build a new community, learn new styles of writing, and perhaps one day, speak publicly in new ways that make a difference.

You can do all of those things. You just have to get your work, and yourself, out there.

You might also struggle with fear or anxiety about stepping into the public sphere. Those feelings are perfectly valid. Writing for quiet academic journals is one thing; writing for a widely read magazine is another. What if your words make someone angry? What if the comments section is ugly? Every time I have a piece come out, even after all of these years, I feel a twinge of anxiety. Years ago, when I was new to this work, I felt a lot of it. I worried so much about putting my ideas—my very *self*—out there for public consumption.

You might wonder whether your mental health is worth the work. That is a valid question. My advice is to weigh the benefits and drawbacks, and if your answer is *no*, then find a different path. You do not need to write for the public to be a successful freelance academic.

My doctoral program did a really great job training me to be an expert in an area of study but a poor job training me to share this expertise with the world outside of academia. And the more I thought about it, I realized that if we experts can't share our expertise, then what's the point of being experts?

Remember: just because you write for public venues doesn't mean you must turn your back on academic writing. For me, writing for the public, such as for smart online venues, satisfies my need to investigate and put those investigations into words. And since I'm not trying to get a tenure-track job anymore, I'm not spending my time publishing and presenting research. It's just not for me.

But that doesn't mean academic writing has no purpose beyond earning a tenure-track job that will never come.

After all, as Kendzior writes at the end of her article on the purpose of academic publishing, scholarship for the purpose of gaining an academic job—one you may likely never get, given the odds—means that all of your scholarly work might leave you feeling empty (as I used to feel). But, when you orient your scholarship toward its obvious yet overlooked purpose—furthering human knowledge—its value does not need to be determined by others, because the value lies in the work itself.

FIVE

Epiphany

THE BURDEN OF CREATIVITY FALLS TO US

Three months into my leave of absence from higher education, I had an epiphany.

The epiphany came courtesy of my friend Sara, who gives me all of my epiphanies. The epiphany happened at lunch with Sara, when she spoke some "words" to me. Usually, my brain processes words. Words are a thing my brain can "do" and do well. But, as she was speaking, I couldn't understand what she was saying.

I kept saying, "What?" "What?" "Huh?" and she kept repeating herself in new and different ways, and her palm was twitching like she wanted to bop my head. Okay, maybe I'm imagining the palm part, Sara, but you have to admit you really were wanting to, or at least you were wondering if maybe the beer was affecting me more than it should have.

The point is, I was very resistant to the epiphany at first. I literally (in the literal meaning of the word) could not process the words Sara was saying to me because they seemed so strange and far-fetched.

But Sara stuck with me until the epiphany occurred, and all was well. No bopping.

But enough talking about this epiphany in the hypothetical. Let me tell you what I learned. Because it changed my life.

The Conversation

Just before the epiphany occurred, a law school sent me a recruitment email for a tenured position. The law school is located in a rather cool city, one located clear across the country from where I live with my husband and kids. At first, I was excited to receive the email. But then I realized I couldn't take the job because it is located far away, and my family (my husband) can't move, and anyways I don't want to move. I really love where I live. And I really love the people I live with. Why should I move?

I told all of this to Sara, and she said, "Did you tell them you don't want to move?"

I said, "No."

She said, "Why not?"

I said, "Because."

She said, "Why not?"

I said, "Because."

She said, "Why not?" Then, "Words words I couldn't understand words words I couldn't understand."

I said, "???????????"

And then I had the epiphany.

The Epiphany

So, what Sara actually said to me was this: "I realize that you don't want to move, and therefore you don't want that particular job. So why don't you ask them to make the job into something that you do want?"

I couldn't understand how that would even be possible. I said some nonsense about distance-learning and the American Bar Association distance-learning standards and something else and something else and it all sounded a lot like *blergity-blerg*.

In retrospect, my problem was that I was suffering from a major failure of creativity.

For those of us living freelance academic lives, we don't

have fixed tracks that we must follow. Our tracks are, by necessity, only limited by our own creativity. They literally (there's that word again) are what we make them.

When we're confronted with a job offer or a gig that isn't quite right for us, instead of turning it down outright (like I did when I received that job offer), we have an opportunity to make the job right—through negotiation or other tactics. We have the opportunity to ask our counterparts to reconfigure what they're asking us to do so that we no longer have any of the worries or concerns that are holding us back from doing work we might be interested in.

But—and this is the hard part—we often have to make a request that is so far off the regular track that no one would ever think of it. I couldn't even figure out how to have a conversation with a friend about the kind of job that I could reimagine that job to be. In law, for example, distance-learning at that time was so new and unusual that I couldn't even imagine a job in which I only commuted to the location every-other-week, say, and taught remotely the rest of the time. I couldn't even figure out how to suggest such a position to the institution that contacted me. My brain had been so well-trained that it couldn't drive off of the well-traveled path and create a new one. What was the likelihood that the people making the job offer could come up with creative solutions when I could not? Likely nil.

So: the burden of creativity on us is really high. But just because we have the burden of creativity doesn't mean we can't ask for the things that will make it possible for us to do the work we love to do.

We Can Bend Reality

I have a friend who is a professor of medicine, a faculty member at a major medical center, a mom, and an entrepreneur. She is, in her way, a freelance academic.

Recently, she said "no" to a last-minute, awesome interview

with a major TV station in New York because she wanted to spend a rare afternoon with her kids. The interview would not have taken long, but arranging childcare and interrupting her day with her children would have been too difficult.

Probably. It seemed. To her.

Plus, the TV people needed her right then. (Welcome to television, apparently. Not that I would know anything about that.)

When she told me about her dilemma, later, and asked me for advice, I drew on my new epiphany. I told her this: "Next time, you can say yes. But you say it like this: 'Yes, awesome. Love to be on TV as an expert. You have an intern to watch my kids for 30 minutes, right?'"

She was like, "That's brilliant. The TV people would never have thought to provide childcare—even for twenty minutes—so I have to think of it for them." She didn't think they would have minded in the slightest. They would have been glad to have provided the childcare to have her on as a last-minute expert, in fact. But the problem was that no one thought of the solution. The problem was a failure of creativity.

For my friend, that failure of creativity won't happen again.

Yes, the burden of creativity lies on those of us who take alternate tracks. But we have more power than we think we do to bend reality in our favor. We just have to start letting clients (including academic institutions) know what we need to get the job done.

If you need help coming up with creative solutions, you aren't alone. Reach out to your freelance academic colleagues and ask for help. If you have a coach who helps you, ask them. It is likely that you aren't the first one to face the particular challenge that you are facing. Ask for some creative brainstorming help. I wish I'd spoken to Sara before I'd turned down that job offer. My doctor friend wishes she'd called me before she'd turned down that TV interview.

Next time we need to bend reality in our favor, let's help each other do it.

SIX

Negative Capability

CRITIQUING AND LOVING HIGHER EDUCATION

As I walked to my local coffeeshop one November morning to write, I saw a daytime moon. I quickly snapped a photo with my phone. The sun was, at the same time, very bright—in the photograph you can see the blueness of the sky, a spectacular, crisp blue that we only get in North Carolina after the summer's humidity has been chased away by cold.

I've lived in North Carolina off and on for most of my life, and I love it here. And I've lived in the Durham/Chapel Hill area off and on since 1994, and I really love it here in particular. I met my husband in Durham, and we're raising our kids in Chapel Hill. If I weren't so unsure about Western religion, I would completely buy into the "Southern Part of Heaven" thing they say around here when bragging about how beautiful things are.

When I saw this morning's daytime moon, with the sun and the moon both brightly visible in the sky at the same time, I thought about a person's ability to feel two ways about a thing at the same time.

This feeling-two-ways does happen, and it happens more often than we think. Keats called it "negative capability." On social media, Cornel West described it this way: "The ability to contemplate the world without the desire to try & reconcile contradictory aspects or fit it into closed & rational systems."[1]

You could just call this way of thinking "being open-minded," but maybe that's too simple.

Here's the point, though. I love Chapel Hill. I love The University of North Carolina at Chapel Hill. I'm a light-blue-blooded Tar Heel.

At the same time, though, I'm ashamed and horrified by the academic-athletic scandal going on at UNC right now, a scandal that is so complex and saddening and yet motivated by good and —at the same time—by the not-good—that it's hard to wrap your head around it unless you're in the middle of it.[2] I'm also bummed out by how the university is corporatizing its administration and killing its tenure lines and transforming its faculty jobs into contingent ones. I'm bummed that UNC drove me from the career I chose by making my job untenable, even though I'd worked to prepare myself to do that job for a decade.

I can feel both ways at the same time: love, and dismay. It's a thing that is possible.

My husband and I are both lifetime alumni association members of UNC. We are basketball season ticket holders. We take our kids to play on the quad and tell them stories about the old buildings—and the slaveowners whom they're named after. We're proud to have attended school here. I'd be proud to have my kids attend school here—and, at the same time, I hope those buildings will all have different names by then. [Update: They do, now.[3]]

As a critic of higher education, I've been accused of hating higher education. Of "trashing" it. But here's my question for you, my readers, and for those like me who write about higher education: Why on earth would I take time to critique higher education if I didn't care so much about making it better for everyone? For students—first and foremost—and for faculty, staff, and everyone who is a part of this extremely valuable public good?

I wouldn't. My mission is to make things better. If some dirty secrets get aired, you may have heard what Supreme Court Justice Brandeis once said about sunlight being the best disinfectant.[4] I'm doing the best I can with that mission in mind.

As a freelance academic, I do my work straddling two worlds: academia, and the world "adjacent to academia," as professor and higher education advocate Raul Pacheco-Vega puts it.[5] Sometimes that adjacent-to-academia world is at peace with higher education; sometimes it isn't. Sometimes my job is to help freelance academics see that they can work smoothly with institutions; sometimes my job is to show freelance academics how institutions do not have their best interests at heart. Usually, my job is to reveal that both can be true—at the same time.

SEVEN

Losing My Affiliation

HOW TO PLAN AHEAD IF YOU'RE PLANNING TO LEAVE

MY ONE YEAR OF UNPAID LEAVE WAS SUPPOSED TO LAST UNTIL THE end of the academic year in May. But I really like my direct supervisor at my institution, and I wanted him to have adequate time to hire my replacement. So as soon as I was sure I wouldn't be returning to my position, I let him know in mid-January.

I did not expect to have my university affiliation—and everything that affiliation entails—cut off within twenty-four hours of giving notice. I thought I would have more time—six more months, until the end of my leave, in fact—to transition away from my institution and, most important, to build a new professional identity.

Instead, I had to do it all in a day and a half.

I'm not complaining, not really. The life of the freelance academic is one I chose. But during that rubber-meets-road moment, I missed the "academic" part of that phrase a lot.

Ever since I started graduate school, I've been a "freeway flyer," teaching at multiple campuses during the same semester (sometimes in different cities). But I always had at least one affiliation, that is, at least one university credential. And being a part of an institution for over a decade gives you access to a lot of things that you don't know you will miss until they're suddenly gone.

Many of the challenges I've encountered during this sudden transition were surprising. Even more surprising were the solutions that I discovered. So in this chapter, I'll share my adventures in suddenly starting over, in the hope that they might help you in your journey from academically employed to self-employed, from academic to freelance academic.

The Easy Stuff

Technology: My institution provided me with a laptop, which was really great. But then I had to turn it in with very little notice—like, only hours. I had been planning for that eventuality, just not so soon. I know that other contingent faculty living closer to the bone would have felt a sudden loss of technology more than I did. But ever since a public-records debacle rocked my institution, I'd been transitioning to my own gear for privacy reasons. I moved all my personal email to a personal email account, and I moved my personal files to a personal hard drive. I had my institutional hard drive regularly backed up to a cloud service, and so when it was time to hand over the laptop, I was ready. I purchased a used laptop, and I moved on.

Library access: Losing library privileges really set me back. I'm still working out the best way to replace that. When I lost library access, I had two journal articles in the editorial process for forthcoming publication. Losing my library access overnight meant that I could no longer check citations or update research.

I immediately reached out to a wonderful librarian (is there any other kind?) at my former institution's library and begged for her help. She reassured me that I could always come into the library and do research in person, using the databases there. Of course, I will no longer have offsite access to those databases, so in that way I'm kind of sunk.

I have one plea to all of you in the freelance academic

community: Share your own research on open-access databases or websites that you control, as I describe earlier in this book. I have shared all of my research on the Social Science Research Network (SSRN). Posting all of your research on your personal website is great—but SSRN is indexed in search engines. Posting your work on SSRN means that anyone like me, who does not have a library password, can access and cite your research.

The Hard Stuff

A university affiliation has been a part of my identity and my job title since I was in my mid-twenties. Losing it was the most amorphous of the challenges I've been facing, and, for a variety of reasons, the hardest one to deal with. That affiliation came up at least a dozen times in the first few days after I lost it. Immediately, I had to face the following tangible challenges:

Email signature: I had to figure out what to put there after I no longer had an affiliation. I had to accept that my work identity would be constantly evolving, and that's okay.

Online presence: I had to update my social media presence. I also began to ask myself, Why, for the love of egg salad, are there so many of these websites to change, and are they all worth it? I had to update my personal website and online C.V. to show my new status as a self-employed person. These website updates were something I hadn't been prepared to do yet. I didn't really have a title, or a business name, or even a job or business description.

Business cards: I had to throw away a box full of university business cards, and then design and order new ones. What should be my logo? What should be my job title? As Admiral James Stockdale put it in the Vice-Presidential Debate of 1992, "Who am I? Why am I here?"[1]

Business structure: I had to incorporate my business and create a retirement account. I now have an S-Corp in the state where I live, and an individual 401(k) plan through that corporation. I rolled my former institution's retirement account into my new company's individual 401(k), as I describe later in this book. Listen, this took a lot of work, and it's still not done yet. Remember: I thought I would have more time.

And those were just the tangible challenges.

Then came the intangibles: I had books that I'd signed contracts to write, so I had to email my editors and tell them I was no longer employed by a university. I was afraid to write these emails: Would my editors be disappointed? Would they kill my contracts? (Answer: no.)

Obviously, I also needed to come up with a new job title that makes sense to other people. Then, I had talks that I was already scheduled to give at conferences—four, in fact. All of those conference name tags and programs were going to state my old institution. I was not looking forward to the awkward conversations that I would have with people after I struck out my institution's name—and do what? Leave the name tag blank? I needed to prepare an explanation, a description, *an identity*.

Because that's what happened. I suddenly lost an identity. That's the heart of the matter, isn't it?

And lastly, there were the intangibles that I wouldn't be able to predict. For example, how much would a loss of affiliation hurt my job prospects in the near future? If I had had time to ramp up my freelance work, to cultivate relationships and clients while still employed, would I have had an easier time transitioning from affiliated academic to unaffiliated freelance academic? At this point, I can only guess.

I can leave you with this: losing your affiliation will never be easy, no matter how much time you have to plan. I get emails from friends and strangers asking how hard it was to quit—and I tell them the same thing. At some point, you just have to do it. You can prepare, and you should, and then, one day, you must go.

EIGHT

Reason to Believe

SETBACKS HAPPEN

WRITING IS BOTH EASY AND HARD.

For some people, writing can be very, very hard. For instance, one of my children has a language acquisition (LA) learning disability that makes writing words and reading them difficult. For me, writing words has never been hard, even when I was very young. Being the mother of a child with an LA disability, a disability so different from my own abilities and disabilities, has forced me to reckon with what I take for granted.

I take for granted that I will be able to put my thoughts into words, words that others will understand, indeed, that others will enjoy reading. One step further: I take for granted that others will enjoy reading my words so much they will pay actual money for me to write those words. Editors pay me and publishers pay me. I'm a professional writer.

For years, now, I've taken for granted that I would write things, and other people would pay me for it.

And then, this week, two years after leaving my steady job in higher education to work full time as a writer, that changed.

At the moment, I'm at a turning point in my career, one that has me feeling uncertainty for the first time in a while—not the ordinary kind of uncertainty that I often feel as a person with anxiety disorder. Not the day-to-day kind. This is the big-picture kind of uncertainty. The step-back-and-reassess my life's purpose kind.

Two years ago, I took a year off from academia to sell a novel. I didn't tell anyone this goal at the time, except my husband. The goal seemed too far-fetched. But I succeeded: I sold the novel, and then the following year, I sold another one. And then, this week, my publisher cut me loose, telling me they didn't want my third novel. When I received the email, I was out with my sister. I glanced at the phone, and my life changed.

As anyone in publishing will tell you, publishers turn out writers all the time. That's a part of publishing. In fact, getting fired by my publisher could be considered a rite of passage for me as a novelist.

It felt awful, though. They weren't closing the press. They just didn't want me. I mourned the work I'd done for them, and the relationships I thought I'd built. And, of course, getting fired called everything I'd done into question. I blamed myself. There was only one conclusion, of course. I was a terrible writer.

People with anxiety and depression are familiar with rumination. It is "a mode of responding to distress that involves repetitively and passively focusing on symptoms of distress and on the possible causes and consequences of these symptoms."[1] The brain plays on repeat all of the awful thing that happened, all of the possible reasons why it might have happened, and all of the awful things that are going to happen now. And you can't make it stop. Rumination is not helpful; in fact, it makes everything worse. You spin yourself in circles about the awful thing until you spiral down to a dark, dark place.

After I finished spinning myself in circles about getting fired by my publisher, I realized I was in much worse trouble than I could have imagined. Because I couldn't write. At all.

But I've been thinking about what it means to be where I am now, a novelist with no home for my books, and I think that maybe, it means nothing at all.

Maybe I should take fewer things for granted, like the fact I have two published novels. Two novels are *not nothing*.

Maybe I should take a legal training course on current topics in disability law and take on a pro bono case.

Maybe I should finish that memoir manuscript that has been teaching me how easy it is to write novels.

Maybe having two children with greater-than-ordinary differences means that I need to cut myself some slack.

Maybe a trip up to the mountains is just what I need, even if it is for work.

Maybe writing is harder than I think it is, and that's okay.

Maybe what I need is a reason to believe, and a reason can be something as small as my kid's smile, or a stormy day.[2]

Maybe, in the end, that's what we all need.

NINE

Bridging Academia

IT IS POSSIBLE TO STRADDLE TWO WORLDS

When I left academia three years ago, I definitely had some guilt about letting my Ph.D. "go to waste." To make things worse, I'm a dual-degree holder—as a former law professor, I also have a J.D. and am a member of the bar. And since I wasn't leaving academia to go into law practice (at least not full time), it was hard not to feel that, in quitting my teaching position, I was dumping nearly a decade of education down the plumbing.

Not a day goes by that I don't see my decision to leave higher education as the right one. No more trying to overlook the antics of a two-tiered system in which tenured and tenure-track faculty (not me) are compensated well, while contingent faculty (hey, that's me) are not, even though the latter do most of the teaching. My anxiety about work decreased: No more worrying about whether one bad course evaluation would get me fired. No more worrying about job security, period.

I have different worries now, but they aren't tied to the frustrating realities of contingent academic life. Today, if certain work is causing me undue stress or anxiety, then I cut it out of my life.

But what about all of those years that I spent training for an academic career? I trained my mind to work in a certain way. I trained myself to have certain skills. I worked hard to develop a C.V. And then I threw it away. Or did I?

When I was contemplating leaving my contingent faculty job, I wrote a five-point manifesto to guide my new career path. When things got confusing, the manifesto made things easier. In the manifesto, I gave myself five basic principles: (1) Get paid for your work. (2) Live in a place you love with the people you love. (3) Stop applying to academic jobs. (4) Remember that you are not alone. (5) When you find yourself being lured back to your department for a temporary gig, remember: They're never going to let you in the club.

In retrospect, writing that manifesto was the beginning of the end of my traditional academic career. Sure, I told myself that if the "perfect" tenure-track job just happened to fall in my lap, I wouldn't turn it down. But we all know that perfect tenure-track jobs do not magically manifest in people's laps. They don't magically manifest at all. You can debate whether academia is a lottery, a merit system, a nepotism system, or a combination of all three, but what it isn't is generous.

So I wrote my manifesto, and I backed away, building a new career adjacent to academia with each backward step.

Then one day, I realized I wasn't backing away from something anymore. I was moving forward, with academia firmly in the rear-view mirror. After eleven years of teaching, I'd finally disentangled myself from that world.

Now I work for me. I own a company, one that's incorporated, and I make a living doing what I do.

But after three years out of higher education, I faced a bit of an identity crisis. I wondered: Can I still call myself a "freelance *academic*"? Sure, I teach the occasional continuing-education course in creative writing at the local university, but I'm not in academia. Not anymore.

I wanted to know: What does it mean to be a freelance academic when you're no longer an academic?

Political scientist and higher education advocate Raul Pacheco-

Vega recently referred to my role as "adjacent-to-academia," and I think that description fits best.[1] I've realized that thinking of myself as "adjacent" has also helped me realize that my years in academia weren't wasted at all. In fact, it turns out that a post-academic career like mine can serve as a bridge between the academy and the nonacademic world—and in a great many ways. And serving as a bridge can have many positive effects.

The most obvious effect, for me, is the work I do regularly: writing for popular audiences to help create an understanding of ideas that are often locked away in the ivory tower. Researchers in higher education create a wealth of knowledge, yet so much of it never reaches audiences outside of academia's narrow silos. Lots of scholars have started sharing their own work and that of others for readers of popular media outlets. I urge everyone to give it a try. I give advice for how to do so later in this book.

Post-academic career coaches help former academics looking to transition out of academia. For those making such a career switch, having a coach—a bridge-tender, if you will—can be crucial to making that transition successfully.

There are many other ways to bridge academia—as a freelance editor, as an admissions coach, as a textbook author, and more. If you've left higher education with your training in your back pocket, you haven't thrown anything away. You've prepared yourself well for a life of your own design.

PART II
Labor Conditions in Higher Education

TEN

Quit Lit Is About Labor Conditions

THE DISMAL STATE OF THE ACADEMIC LABOR MARKET HAS BEEN critiqued for years. Those of us who began our doctorates before contingent labor had become the norm, back when there were still jobs to be had, finished our doctorates with little hope for a career in sight. So we worked as contingent faculty. We usually made very little money. We had no job security. Some of us left, and some of us who left then wrote about it.

These essays about leaving academia became a genre, and the genre gained a name: "Quit Lit."

The Quit Lit Foremothers

Higher education critic Rebecca Schuman wrote an early piece of quit lit in 2013, titled "Thesis Hatement," in which she warns readers to avoid higher education.[1] She warns them not to go to graduate school: "Don't do it. Just don't." She tells them why: "I now realize graduate school was a terrible idea because the full-time, tenure-track literature professorship is extinct." She also describes the pain she suffered as she trained for a career that was never going to manifest: "During graduate school, you will be broken down and reconfigured in the image of the academy. By the time you finish—if you even do—your academic self will be the culmination of your entire self, and thus you will believe, incomprehensibly, that not having a tenure-track job makes you worthless." These three arguments—warning, critique, and description of one's suffering—comprise the heart of all quit lit. Not every essay has all three arguments, but all essays have at least one.

One of the most attractive qualities about Schuman's essay is that she doesn't hedge. She doesn't say that there are "fewer" jobs. She says that there are no jobs. Because, as she points out, in her discipline there were one hundred and fifty applicants a year for six positions world-wide. With those numbers, the difference between few and none is no difference at all.

Despite its grimness, Schuman's essay is inspiring as well. She inspired me to write and publish my first non-scholarly essay as I was inching toward the exit of higher ed. The essay I wrote described the litany of the tiny, daily humiliations of being a contingent faculty member (and it serves as the prologue to this book). But, in retrospect, that piece was also setting up the evidence that I would use when I finally quit. I was able to point to that essay to prove why life as contingent faculty in the contemporary university is, for the most part, as untenable as Schuman described. It was worth quitting.

I quit, and I wrote about it. I also connected with other writers who wrote about quitting around the same time I did—with Schuman, Kelly J. Baker, Sarah Kendzior, Elizabeth Keenan, and others. We wrote about the terrible experiences of being contingent in academia. We were mocked for doing so, sometimes, by people both inside and outside academia. We were told to "stop complaining"—either our poor job situation was our own fault (people inside the academy usually said this) or we didn't have it so bad (people outside the academy usually said this). We had a variety of goals, sometimes simultaneously: to help others make better decisions than we did (don't go!) and to improve academia with thoughtful critique.

We were mostly women—because, as Kelly J. Baker points out in her book *Sexism Ed*, contingent faculty are predominantly women.[2] We are mommy-tracked. We are trailing spouses. Although we are hard workers, we are not "brilliant" like men are, as Baker puts it, so therefore we don't deserve tenure-track jobs.

Over the years, my quit lit friends have gone separate ways and found success in their new chosen fields: journalism, writing, real estate, and more. The fire that drove us away from the academy in the days of the rise of contingent faculty—and the attendant rise of quit lit—had cooled to a slow burn. Because that's what drove quit lit in the beginning. Quit lit, at its heart, was a labor critique.

Insider Quit Lit

Five years pass. In 2018, the *Chronicle of Higher Education* published a new quit lit essay by contingent history faculty Erin Bartram, who spent five years failing to get a tenure-track job. The essay garnered tens of thousands of readers. Titled "Why Everybody Loses When Someone Leaves Academe," the essay opens with Bartram's final failure on the academic job market. As she leaves her office for the last time, she describes it with all the nostalgia the cliché of a professor can muster, including a reading lamp and fountain pen ink.

Then her essay takes a surprising turn. Her indictment is not one of the dismal labor market created by the institutional problems of higher education. Instead, she critiques her field (or any field) that allows the loss of scholarly colleagues to continue unabated, colleagues whose contributions to research will be lost forever. She writes, "Even in our supportive responses to those leaving, we don't want to face what's being lost." Later she writes, "We don't want these people to go, and we don't want to lose all the ideas floating around in their heads, so we say, 'Please give us those ideas, at least. Please stay with us just a little bit.'" And she's right; when I left academia, my former colleagues said similar things to me.

Like Schuman, she talks about the pain of losing the part of her identity that she trained years to build: "I've lost a huge part of my identity, and all of my book-learning on identity construction can't help me now." And perhaps most poignantly: "I don't know what I'm going to do. I don't know what I'm good for."

Bartram's piece, oddly, "generated a vesuvian outpouring of responses."[3] The essay was read "at least eighty thousand times."[4] By any metric, Bartram's piece struck a chord with readers. But who was reading it?

Her essay appeals to outsiders who have quit academia. But Bartram's piece is radically unlike Schuman's and other quit lit in a particular way that makes it appealing to more than just those who have been forced out of the academy. It is not a labor critique. She does not discuss the exploitative academic labor market and the role that her (beloved) tenured colleagues play in upholding that exploitation. It does not describe poor working conditions—on the contrary, her conditions seem to have been good. She had an office, and a desk, and a lamp. She had colleagues that she will miss. Perhaps her conditions were poor like those of most contingent faculty, but those poor conditions are not described in this essay.

Because her essay does not provide a labor critique, it appeals to insiders, those on the tenure-track and others who approve of the higher ed status quo (the status quo that harmed Bartram herself). Instead, her essay is full of nostalgia for the academy. This nostalgia does not appear in Schuman's essay and most other quit lit. Bartram doesn't speak to how working as contingent faculty can be back-breaking and poverty-inducing. She speaks to how much she'll miss her research and her chosen field, not to how much she was pushed out by those who stay behind—by that field itself.

Indeed, weirdly, she still speaks of her chosen field as though she were a part of it and not the one leaving. She uses the first-person plural "we": "We don't want these people to go, and we don't want to lose all the ideas floating around in their heads." In this essay, Bartram (whether intentionally or no), still frames herself as an insider. No wonder the essay was so appealing to so many. Although buried in her essay was a strong message of suffering, she did not put the blame where it belongs. Instead, she comforts the colleagues who benefit from the system that pushed her out: "What would happen if we, as a community, stopped saying 'he's gone to a better place,' bringing a casserole, and moving on. What would happen if we acknowledged the losses our discipline suffers every year? What would happen if we actually grieved for those losses?" As I read the piece, I wondered, *Does she even know why she lost her job? Does she want to hold those people and systems accountable?* Bartram's essay was not quit lit. On the contrary, it was an encomium of higher education, and higher education loved it.

A Practical Labor Critique

If quit lit is about labor, then the best quit lit published in 2018 wasn't about quitting at all. Annemarie Pérez's essay, "Instead of Gaslighting Adjuncts, We Could Help Them," described how a contingent faculty's current department can do practical, material things to help that faculty member further their academic career instead of continuing to exploit them.[5] Pérez's piece was one of the few things I've read recently that still burned with fire about the dismal academic job market and the attendant labor exploitation.

Quit lit does not tend to have the happy ending that Pérez's essay has—she landed a tenure-track job after many years as contingent faculty and with the mentorship she found in her temporary department. Other pieces over the years have had a very different outcome: faculty, usually contingent faculty, have left the academy, disillusioned by the mistreatment they experienced in the departments that exploited them.

But don't be fooled: Pérez's essay is an indictment all the same. The essay provides a practical guide for tenured faculty who work alongside contingent faculty. Pérez pulls no punches: "We don't have to just wring our hands about how terrible the situation is, or, worse still, say the job market has always been terrible and those who are adjuncts should never have started a Ph.D. if they weren't willing to be exploited." Instead, she says, mentor, guide, help. The jobs are there, actually, if you are willing to help instead of pretending not to see.

Those people in Bartram's essay who bring casseroles? Those are the people Pérez is taking aim at.

Bartram's piece had heart. But in the end, it coddled the powerful. Pérez's piece called them on their gaslighting and provided concrete steps for fixing the problem my friends and I have been writing about for five years. But eighty thousand people haven't read Pérez's piece because it isn't an encomium of the academy.

The academy doesn't need encomiums or casseroles. It needs practical labor critiques like Pérez's. And it still needs quit lit, stories from marginalized higher education faculty who, because of career change or some other reason, finally have the ability to tell them. If you are getting started as a freelance academic, perhaps the first thing you should write is your good-bye letter. Even if you never share it with anyone but yourself.

ELEVEN

The University Is Just Another Client

WHEN YOU'RE A CONTINGENT FACULTY MEMBER, IT IS IN AN institution's best interest to get you to do the most work for the least amount of money. You have a transactional relationship. It can be hard, when you're the faculty member, to think of your job that way, when we've all been trained, through years of graduate school, to think of higher education as a calling, rather than as a job. But when you're contingent, that's exactly what you have—a job.

In fact, when you're contingent, you often don't even have a job. You have a gig.

Contingency has turned higher education into just another part of the gig economy. It's a sad state of affairs, but it's here to stay.

Many times, I've had some form of a conversation I'm about to describe with contingent faculty colleagues—and even some tenure-track ones—about university power dynamics and how to use them.

Here's a typical situation.

Early on a Tuesday morning, I'm having coffee with my friend Elle. She's been searching high and low for a way to break through the contingent ceiling at our institution. She is teaching on a nonrenewable contract in the same division where I used to teach, and she wants to find a way to get our division to hire her on a permanent basis when her contract expires.

With that goal in mind, she has taken on more service work. She has taken on an extra course for no extra pay. And she is letting more students into the classes she already teaches. She's doing all of this extra labor hoping that someone in a position of authority will recognize how awesome she is.

I'm stunned by how much extra work she is doing. I have to consciously force myself to just ask questions (and no, not leading questions), to get a full sense of just how many hours a week she spends doing work beyond her actual job.

Finally, I ask, "Why are you doing all of this extra work?"

And finally, she says, "I really want them to keep me on after my contract ends."

There is so much hope, and pain, in her voice, that I want to give her a hug. But I refrain. She doesn't need a hug. She needs someone to tell her that our division is *never* going to renew her contract.

But is she going to believe me? A year before, I was just another contingent faculty member. But when I was in similar shoes as hers, overworking myself, hoping these same people would let me jump over to the tenure track, I did a very scary thing and asked our division head if I would ever be permitted to do so.

He told me I would not. Worse, he insulted me for even asking.

Bursting that bubble hurt, but it also cleared my vision.

Sitting with Elle, I know she needs to ask the hard question. I can't answer it for her. She needs to pull aside her supervisor and say, directly, "Is there any chance my contract will be renewed?" And when they say "no," she needs to spend less time giving the institution her lifeblood and spend more time on herself.

The moral of the story is this: if you are contingent faculty, overworking yourself will rarely pay off. If you aren't sure, you need to find out. And don't worry—asking won't hurt your chances. Your department might prefer to keep you in the dark in order to get your free labor, but getting the truth will only help your career.

Years ago, my friend Elle was doing the contingent faculty equivalent of writing a piece for a magazine on spec. "On spec" is a journalism term that refers to when editors ask newbie journalists to write pieces prior to buying them. Usually that's not how it works. Usually, you pitch a piece, the editor accepts it, and then you write it. Usually you don't do the work not knowing whether you'll be paid.

What Elle described was even worse than writing on spec because she wasn't talking about one article, she was talking about her whole career.

As a contingent faculty member, you work your whole career on spec. Every class you teach, every grant you write, every article you publish—they're all on spec, because you have no job security to back you up if a project doesn't pan out. You work and work, hoping some person in authority will give you: (a) more money, (b) more job security, (c) more job respect, or some combination of (a), (b), and (c).

But then it never pans out. As those of us who've been at this for a while know, giving administrators your work for free does not inspire them to reward you. More frequently, doing the extra work backfires and inspires administrators to turn your previously volunteered work into new job requirements. Suddenly what you did as a favor becomes a rigid job expectation. Soon, you're on the path to overwork, burnout, depression, and worse.

Fortunately, I have a solution. It begins with a shift of mindset—from that of employee to that of freelancer. As a freelancer, your institution is just one of your many clients. That means you need to spend your extra time and energy on projects that earn you both money and respect outside of one particular institution.

You know who works on spec a lot? Freelancers. But they

(usually) know how to do it while preserving their time, finances, and mental health.

Contingent faculty are the freelancers of academia, and we need to start acting like it. Look at it this way: Your university has basically already said that you are a freelancer. You are already working job to job—gig to gig. That's what a short-term contract means. Or in the case of my friend, a terminal contract: She took a job with a client, and when that job ended, so did the client relationship.

Fine.

But if that is the case, then your institution will just be one of your many clients. Freelancers don't make a living hoping one client will keep hiring them over and over. They form other relationships; they find other clients. Contingent faculty need to do the same. And if you are a tenure-track professor reading this, and you have noticed that higher education might not be able to sustain you either, then I'm also talking to you. It's time for all of us in higher education to diversify.

So instead of giving away your work for free, hoping for a reward—financial and emotional—that will never come, embrace the freelancer ethos. Take some of your time back to work for yourself.

Often when I suggest that we should apply this client-based strategy to academia, however, I get pushback. For some people, this strategy seems disloyal to their institution—like you're cheating on your significant other. But you can only be loyal to a company that is loyal to you. And if you are contingent faculty, your institution is rarely going to be loyal to you.

In order to make time for yourself, you'll need to dial back the "adjunct heroics," as writer and former professor Rebecca Schuman has put it.[1] That is exactly the advice that I would give my friend: Decline unpaid service work that won't be rewarded anyway. Keep office hours to the minimum requirement. Set limits on your letters of recommendations for students. And deflect all the guilt that others will probably lay on you—guilt from faculty, from students, and even from yourself.

It took me a while to adjust to the freelance academic mindset. I really, really wanted to feel loyalty to all of the institutions where I worked. I wanted to find a home. But each time, the same thing happened: I was told, directly and indirectly, in large and small ways, that I did not belong. I felt betrayed and hurt. I cried, a lot. (You are probably very stoic and do not cry. I'm happy for you.) When these slights and put-downs and exploitations started happening at my final institution, I didn't feel like I'd been hoodwinked. I felt like I'd made the same dumb mistake again, and I blamed myself. I felt ashamed.

So I picked myself up, and I changed my mindset completely. Changing my mindset was hard. It was "hanging up on a calling," as Schuman puts it.[2] It was recognizing that a career I'd trained for years to do was no longer going to be my career. It meant letting go of shame, which was hard but also freeing.

I couldn't quit outright—my family needed my salary. But I was ready to start planning an exit strategy. And I was ready to start making my life better immediately, before I quit. Enter the freelance mindset. My institution, I decided, was just another client.

Say you've adjusted your mindset. You're ready. Your institution is Client A. But it's time to look around for other clients, too. Who else is there?

Think about which of your skills are marketable. Sit down and write a list of every possible skill that you have. This is not the time to be humble. You might not know who to market your skills to, or how, but that's OK. You can start learning those things. You're an academic. You know how to research.

First transform your C.V. into a résumé—or various résumés for different types of work you might be interested in doing. When I did this myself, it was—and I'm not kidding—so much fun. I used Rachel Leventhal-Weiner's article on résumé writing for academics for guidance ("Don't Fear the Résumé").[3] If you try to make your skills list and your résumé and have trouble—a totally understandable problem—hire a post-academic coach to help you figure out what you're good at that can earn money.

Most important, at least for your mental health, recognize that you are not alone. Build a community, whether online or off, of others who are trying to do work similar to yours. That community will help you network into new opportunities and will reassure you when you start to doubt yourself. There are freelance networking communities that you can join. I subscribe to a newsletter called, unsurprisingly, *The Freelancer*, which helped me learn about setting rates, dealing with clients, and more. And you can join the Freelancers Union to learn even more about the practical side of freelance life. They even have health and other kinds of insurance for their members.

Remember that moving into the mindset of a freelance academic does not mean that you give up your job teaching on a campus. It just means that you approach your relationship with your institution differently. You no longer belong to them: They belong to you. Once that shift happens—and you'll know when it does—there's nothing more empowering.

TWELVE

The Ugly Side of Academia

IT'S NOT SOUR GRAPES. IT'S WAKING UP.

I WORKED IN ACADEMIA FOR ELEVEN YEARS. IF YOU COUNT MY master's program, when I had to fend off harassment by two different tenured male professors, and law school, when my favorite tenure-track professor was denied tenure for being a woman and another tenured male professor (who was in his sixties) married one of my classmates (who was in her twenties), even longer.

Recently, I came across some words by James Baldwin: "The price one pays for pursuing any profession, or calling, is an intimate knowledge of its ugly side."[1] He touches on how those who are marginalized and oppressed know a lot more about those in power than those in power know about those who are marginalized and oppressed. And Baldwin does it the way Baldwin does—with precise, cutting, yet lyrical language that flips your world upside-down.

The point is, I've pursued this profession of higher education for most of my professional life. And, because of my experiences —as a woman, as a disabled woman, as a disabled woman in a slew of contingent positions—I can see that this profession is really ugly. But I'm wondering, today, is academia any uglier than any other profession? Or do I just see its ugly side because I am so intimate with academia? And further, does everyone in academia see academia's ugly side?

Is it possible for a straight, white, cismale tenured professor at a top university to jamble along and never ever see the ugliness of academia the way that marginalized faculty do? For it to actually not be ugly for them at all?

The other day, a tenured, straight, white, cismale professor in my division actually asked one of my contingent colleagues how much we earned because he had no idea. Now, I know how much this tenured white male professor makes—because we worked at a public university, and all of our salaries are public record. Once upon a time, I took that public data and created a spreadsheet to compare salaries by race and sex. The results, as you might imagine, were not surprising. Women and people of color make less money. We are also overrepresented in the contingent ranks.

I would never, however, have had the gall to ask a tenured professor what his salary was. I also would have been afraid of being fired.

When this tenured professor learned what the contingent faculty earn each year, he dropped an f-bomb out of shock. The professor just had never considered that we would be paid so little for all the work that we do. It was his privilege to never think about it. Whereas for the rest of us, we have to think about money all the time because we frequently make so little.

So I think that yes, contingent faculty, and certain others on the tenure-track, like white women who get denied tenure for not being masculine enough, and women of color who get pushed out for not being "respectful" enough (yes, these things happen all the time in top-secret, non-appealable tenure votes), we really do get to see an uglier side of academia.

Because we have to think about it. We're forced to stare the ugly side in the face every day, even as we do our work teaching, writing, counseling students, and trying to make the world a better place.

Recently, a friend I respect told me that my writing critiquing higher education came across as "sour grapes." She felt compelled to bring it up because we are entering into a business endeavor together. And keep in mind, she was sincerely, truly worried about hurting my feelings. Also, you can see her perspective: Is a crank a good spokesperson for your business?

But I was truly surprised that she viewed my words as sour grapes—or as anything that could reasonably be perceived as such—in the first place. I actually think I'm kind of Pollyannaish, once you get past the "we need to stop deluding ourselves" bit. I don't wallow in misery, and I'm very practical. The point of the freelance academic endeavor is not just to identify problems with higher education, but to find ways to fix them as well.

After our conversation, I looked up "sour grapes" in the dictionary. I learned that the phrase derives from one of Aesop's fables, "The Fox and the Grapes." These days, it refers to a situation "in which someone adopts a negative attitude to something because they cannot have it themselves." So I guess my friend is saying (and I'm inferring here) that since I didn't get a tenure-track job, I have sour grapes towards higher education.

But she's wrong. And worse, she's not alone. A friend told me a story where a former colleague, someone tenured but miserable, asked my friend if she were "jealous" of tenured-and-miserable's job. When my friend told me this story, we couldn't believe how, after all of the public writing we've done on leaving higher education, someone could still think we wished that we were tenured in the academy.

No: I feel like I narrowly escaped by not landing a tenure-track job. There's something rotten in the state of higher education, and if I'd moved my family into that dying kingdom, where would I be? Hoarding my meager riches and stomping on contingent faculty? Or worse, pitying contingent faculty and wringing my hands because there is nothing I can do—after all, the problems are structural and too big to fix? I'd probably hate myself—if I were self-aware enough to know what I was doing.

It might help stave off your former colleagues' probing

questions if you can figure out an answer to this one: "What do you do now?" The answer need not be permanent. It can change as your work does.

Answering this question isn't about figuring out how other people see you. It's about figuring out how you see yourself and what you want to be *for yourself*. It gives you confidence.

I know one thing for certain: I do not want to be a tenure-track professor.

The academy cannot give me anything that I cannot discover on my own. That's not sour grapes. That's waking up. That's what it means to be a freelance academic.

Later in this book I will address, in a more hopeful fashion, the wonderful open pathways that higher education holds for us. Because that hope is there. Those pathways are there. Thinking creatively about learning, teaching, finding/making/sharing knowledge—we have to do those things. And we can.

Also, we have to eat. I'll talk about that, too.

THIRTEEN

The Invisible Adjunct Hero at Kentucky

HOW HIGHER ED PRIZES CONTINGENT OVERWORK

I RECENTLY READ A NEWS STORY IN WHICH AN UNDERGRADUATE student crawled through an air duct to steal a statistics final in order to cheat at the University of Kentucky.[1] After crawling in, the student let another student into the building, but after they entered the professor's office they were busted by the professor, who was working that night. The students took off running. But when one of them realized that the professor would be able to recognize him in class, he returned and confessed.

The kicker? All of this took place around two a.m. on a Wednesday.

A few things about the story struck me as odd. First, in the article, published in the *New York Times*, the *Times* was very, very careful to never use the word "professor" to refer to the teacher, but rather "instructor": "The instructor at the University of Kentucky, who was working very late, had gone out for a midnight meal and returned just in time to derail the plan, according to a university spokesman."

Second, the late hours of the events struck me as odd as well. Why was the professor at work so late? Obviously, his students didn't expect him to be there. Sometimes professors teach late,

81

when they teach, say, graduate seminars that run into the evenings. But the large, introductory courses for which a student might bother to steal an exam? Those don't usually take place late. And stealing an exam? That's not the sort of thing you do for an upper-level seminar. And no seminar lasts until two a.m.

Someone not attuned to higher education might miss these details. Someone who hadn't spent a career as a contingent faculty member wouldn't make the same deductions I did, deductions it only took a quick internet search to confirm. Of course the "instructor" was a contingent faculty member. Of course he was.

After I conducted a little research, I figured out which course that the students were stealing the exam for: "Statistical Methods and Motivations: Introduction to principles of statistics with emphasis of conceptual understanding." And the professor listed for this course? His name is listed as "TBD." Actually, the professor who busted the students is named John P. Cain—but his name is not on the course listing.

This news story highlights the lives of contingent faculty. We work too much, at wacky hours, often in shared offices, teaching introductory classes over and over again, with courses, schedules, and locations that are perpetually "TBD."

Contingent faculty are the TBD. As Crash Davis put it in the movie *Bull Durham*, we're The Player to Be Named Later.[2]

The heroic instructor at Kentucky was indeed scheduled to teach the summer following the spring he caught those students, and again in the fall. Good for him. At least he has a modicum of job security—even if he does have to teach the exact same course over and over again.

For many contingent faculty, we teach the same course or courses in a cycle of underpaid, mind-numbing work that Sisyphus would run from. Well, maybe not Sisyphus, since he didn't have much of a choice—but neither do many contingent faculty.

Maybe Professor TBD has a full-time position, even. Fingers

The Freelance Academic

crossed. Professor Cain, if you're reading this, I'm rooting for you. However, it doesn't look like he has his own office, from this list of Statistics faculty that I found. His title is "Staff Instructor of Statistics." And although he has an email address, unlike the rest of his cohort, he does not have an office address.

Except—from the story—he seems to have an office—the one that the students broke into. So that means that, although he does have an office (whether his own, or shared), no one at his institution has bothered to update the website with his information, which is completely normal when you are contingent. I was once told that because I was contingent, my name didn't need to be in the faculty directory because I was likely to be gone soon. The point is, Professor Cain's experience is not unique: his invisibility, his TBD-ness. This experience is normal, and normalized, across higher ed. But that doesn't mean it is okay.

But I haven't gotten to the best part of the story yet. The capstone. At the end of the story in the *Times*, the University of Kentucky spokesman Jay Blanton had this to say about the circumstances and his overworked, underpaid academic laborer: "'Cheating and theft of this kind is very serious in an academic institution,' he said, adding that episodes like this were rare at the university's College of Arts and Sciences, which has 10,000 students. 'It's an unusual set of circumstances,' he said. 'It also underscores how late our faculty work.'"

Look, Blanton: There's nothing to be proud of about how late Professor Cain was working. When your underpaid, overworked, contingent faculty are in the building at two o'clock in the morning, you should be ashamed. You should be asking what your institution is doing wrong that your faculty must work at two a.m. in order to get their work done on time. You need to figure out what you can do better so that they can have a reasonable quality of life, instead of one where they work hours that would burn out even the most resilient worker.

You don't brag about the long hours they work in the largest newspaper in the United States. Your bragging shows that the University of Kentucky is just like every other school I've worked at and researched: you don't care about the health and well-being of your contingent faculty at all. Your professor may be a hero, but you have failed.

FOURTEEN

The Racism False Equivalence Strikes Again

PUBLIC ENGAGEMENT IS RISKY FOR VULNERABLE FACULTY

IN JUNE 2017, ESSEX COUNTY COLLEGE IN NEW JERSEY, A community college, fired a Black contingent faculty member named Lisa Durden, because, as the Associated Press reported, "officials say she made racially insensitive comments on Fox News."[1] Durden appeared on *Tucker Carlson Tonight* on June 6. Two weeks later she was out of a job.

Durden appeared on Tucker Carlson's show, and given Tucker's personality, Durden must be a cool-headed woman to go anywhere near a person whose goal in life is to anger rational people and make them lose their cool. Tucker had her on the show to talk about a Black Lives Matter Memorial Day celebration on her campus that was for Black people only.

Tucker, all fake-innocence, wanted to know why white people couldn't go, too, and isn't that racist to have an event for Black people only? He said, "I thought the whole point of Black Lives Matter was to speak out against singling out people based on race? ... Explain that to me."

Durden replied, "What I say to that is, 'Boo-hoo, you white people are angry because you couldn't use your white privilege card to get invited to the Black Lives Matter all-black Memorial Day celebration.' Let me contextualize that for you." At that point in her reply, Tucker started talking over Durden, acting angry at her words.

Honestly, this far into in the conversation about Black Lives Matter, if there are white people who still cannot understand that the purpose of Black Lives Matter is not to stop "singling out people based on race" but rather to point out how Black lives, you know, *matter*, then I don't know what to do. There are only two possible explanations for Tucker's question. Either he is very, very stupid, or he was asking a specious question.

I think he was asking a specious question, that is, a question in bad faith. Black Lives Matter is not about the cessation of singling people out. It's about the cessation of violence against Black bodies. Tucker knew that. His question was intended to rile up his guest.

But none of that matters. At all. I don't have to explain how right-wing talk show hosts use rhetorical fallacies to frustrate conversation. That sort of wordplay is the bread-and-butter of Fox News and its hosts.

The problem here is that a contingent faculty member stepped out of the ivory tower to engage in a public debate. She took a risk in appearing on a right-wing television show. And she lost her job for it.

Two days after the show aired, Essex County College fired Durden, right in the middle of the semester. Never once on the air did she mention that she was affiliated with the college. She also made it clear that all of her views were her own.

But taking care to maintain distance from the college didn't matter to Essex. Her hard work taking a stand as a public intellectual didn't either. They fired her anyway, and they did it, quite openly, because of her speech on Tucker's show. Here's an excerpt from the statement on her firing from Anthony Munroe, Essex County College President: "The character of this institution mandates that we embrace diversity, inclusion, and unity. Racism cannot be fought with more racism."

The "racism begets more racism" argument is a fallacy called "false equivalence," once of the most common of the fallacies. In this story, it appeared twice: in Tucker's "but I thought" nonsense and then in Munroe's use of the old rotten chestnut, "Racism cannot be fought with more racism." Both Tucker and Munroe are saying the same thing: "reverse racism is the same as racism" or "racism done by Black people against white people is the same as racism done by white people." Or however you want to frame it.

A false equivalence is a fallacy that happens you take two opposing viewpoints and claim they are equal—but they aren't. False equivalence is a favorite of people making racist arguments. It was the undergirding of "separate, but equal."[2] And it persists in racist arguments to this day.

"Reverse racism is equivalent to racism" is a false equivalence. Here's the deal: Racism is part of the tidal wave of history, social influence, governmental control, violence, wealth, white supremacy, and everything else that gives white people—*as a group*—power over people of color—*as groups*. In individual interactions, racism plays out in individual ways, sure. But there can be no "reverse racism" until there has been, say, a century or more of racial oppression of white people by Black people.

Tucker's nonsense is literally his schtick: to say offensive things to people who work hard to make the world a better place in order to provoke them. I have no idea how he sleeps at night. Who cares about Tucker. He's a clown.

But I cannot understand how a college president doesn't understand the most basic of logical fallacies. I presume he took freshman composition. I taught that course for a decade, and all of my students walked out of my class knowing how to spot a false equivalence.

But let's say rhetorical fallacies are not Munroe's strong suit. Fine. At the very least, as a college president, Munroe must understand intellectual freedom and the First Amendment. He also should stand by his faculty, especially his most vulnerable faculty, such as a Black woman who is contingent faculty. But instead he threw her under the bus.

Sociologist and higher education critic Tressie McMillan Cottom has written about "how woefully underprepared universities are to deal with the reality of public scholarship, public intellectuals, or public engagement," despite how vociferously they cry for their faculty to engage in public discourse.[3] In particular, she warns, "According to many, colleges are hotbeds for radical anti-white 'reverse racism' and feminist wars on men." Because of this public context, when faculty members engage publicly, there is a tinderbox ready to start fire, and institutions are "woefully underprepared universities are to deal with the reality of public scholarship, public intellectuals, or public engagement." Just as Cottom has observed, Essex County College was unprepared for the outcry of reverse racism, and it didn't stand by its faculty. The college fired her instead.

Durden's situation is one of many reasons why I will never return to higher education, even when friends forward me promising jobs. All of us who are trying to make the world a better place need to be able speak our minds. We can't be, even unconsciously, holding our tongues because we're afraid of getting fired. Some of us, as Durden's experience has shown, don't have another option. But some of us do, and it is our duty to carry that weight.

Unless you are a professor with tenure (and even then) higher education no longer cares about the duty of a professor to "profess"—from the Latin, which means to declare, publicly. Today's university wants automatons who will toe the line of a consumerist model and, most importantly, keep their mouths shut.

Durden wasn't fired because of reverse racism. She was fired because of plain old regular racism. She was a Black, female, contingent professor, one of the most vulnerable members of the professoriate, the most likely to be fired, the most contingent, the most likely to be criticized for being too loud or too disruptive. No one should be surprised that she lost her job. Higher education fails to protect people like her all the time.

But we should all be angry. And then we should take that anger, and we should do something about it. Use your platforms to call attention to stories like this. Stand up for your fellow faculty if you are still in the academy, and for faculty at the institutions where you are alumni. Whatever you do, if you are able to do so, do something.

FIFTEEN

What's Your BATNA?

FINDING LEVERAGE IN NEGOTIATIONS

IN ANY NEGOTIATION, BEING WILLING TO WALK AWAY MEANS THAT YOU essentially have all of the power. Sure, the opposing side might have some things that you wish you had. But in the end, if you don't agree to the terms of the opposing side, and if the opposing side wanted the agreement more, they're the loser.

Here's an example. Most of us were taught, probably by a parent, that the first rule of car buying is to be willing to walk away from a deal you don't like. In my house growing up, walking away was not only the first rule of car buying, but it was also the first and the second rule of car buying. (Our third rule was to never use paint color as a decision-making factor.) Applying the walk-away rule to a car deal puts the power in your hands rather than the dealer's because the dealer *really* wants to sell the car.

Of course not all negotiations are so simple. Among the most difficult are the ones we do in the workplace. And job negotiations in the academic workplace are especially fraught. For contingent faculty, our lack of leverage and job security often means that we have little negotiating power at all. If you are a contingent faculty member at a university without collective bargaining, how can you negotiate more favorable conditions?

BATNA: Best Alternative to a Negotiated Agreement

I don't have a magic answer for fixing the lack of leverage that contingent faculty face, but I have a concept I want to share that helped me with my own negotiations: BATNA. It stands for "best alternative to a negotiated agreement." Thinking in terms of BATNA can make your life off the tenure track—or your transition out of academia—a little more well planned and enjoyable.

The concept of BATNA was first introduced by Roger Fisher and William Ury in their 1981 book on negotiation *Getting to Yes: Negotiating Agreement Without Giving In*. They write, "The reason you negotiate is to produce something better than the results you can obtain without negotiating." They tell you to ask yourself not only "What are those results?" but also "What is that alternative? What is your BATNA—your Best Alternative To a Negotiated Agreement? That is the standard against which any proposed agreement should be measured."[1]

Thus, BATNA is not synonymous with your "bottom line," which, according to negotiation expert David Venter, refers to the "worst possible outcome that a negotiator might accept."[2] You don't want to negotiate with your eye on the bottom line. You want the best alternative, not the worst. If you can't agree with your adversary, you want your BATNA. The function of BATNA, Venter explains, is that "it prohibits a negotiator from accepting an unfavorable agreement or one that is not in their best interests because it provides a better option outside the negotiation." BATNA is the open door that you can run through as soon as you see that your negotiations are going awry. It's your escape route.

So how do you find your BATNA? Professor of law and economics Guhan Subramanian writes that BATNA "is among one of the many pieces of information negotiators seek when formulating dealmaking and negotiation strategies." To figure out your BATNA, Subramanian writes, ask this question: "If your current negotiation reaches an impasse, what's your best outside option?"[3]

As a contingent faculty member, you might not feel like you have many outside options. I get it; I really do. It didn't take long for me to figure out that a career off the tenure track was going to be uncertain. I could feel the anxiety grow inside me when I considered how easily I could lose my job. For my own piece of mind, I needed to take steps to create backup plans and stopgaps. Over time, those stopgaps became a career. One textbook became five. One regular column in a magazine became many. One editing client became a steady stream. One day, I realized I had an outside option. And as time went on, that outside option got better and better.

Over the Barrel

What led me to think about BATNA? I spent eleven years as a contingent employee of various universities. My positions varied widely: I worked at three different universities, in four different divisions, in five different positions off of the tenure track teaching repetitive courses in college writing. Once, I had a job where I started out with a three-year contract. I thought it was going to be fantastic. Then the head of the division called all contingent faculty into a room together and told us that all future contracts would be year-to-year. No more multi-year stability.

We were upset. But there was nothing we could do. After all, a year-to-year job was better than no job, and most of us needed jobs. We had no leverage to demand longer contracts. If we all quit together (which would never have happened anyway, given the particular dynamics of our group), the division head could have easily replaced us with new people desperate for work. We preferred to think that "new people" might not have been as good as we were, but who knows, really. There are many excellent unemployed professors out there.

The Freelance Academic

The division chair had us over a barrel. Having no negotiating power was a terrible feeling.

A few weeks later, the division chair called us into that room again, and this time she told us that not all of our contracts would be renewed the following year. Some of us would have to be cut. The administration, we were told, would be reviewing course evaluations to make the decision of whom to keep and whom to fire.

Once again, we were over a barrel.

At this point, I'd been working in the division for three years without a raise. And there were no raises—not even cost-of-living increases—on the horizon. But how could we ask for raises? We were playing a real-life game of *Survivor* in order to keep our jobs.

If you want to know why contingent faculty unionize, just ask around for stories like that one. They're everywhere in the academy. Broken promises, gameshow-like competitions pitting employees against one another to retain their jobs. When my division chair announced this higher ed version of *Survivor*, I started looking for a new job. I didn't try to negotiate. What would I have negotiated?

Luckily, I landed a contingent job in another division at my same university, one with another three-year contract. I thought things would be better. They weren't. There are some things that will always be problems so long as there are haves (tenure-track faculty) and have-nots (contingents). The tenure-track faculty got paid twice as much as we did to do less work. They had special privileges we would never be offered. And the social interaction was brutal: to the tenured faculty, our names weren't worth learning because we weren't worth knowing.

After three years in this new division, I put in for a promotion to the contingent faculty equivalent of associate professor. I received the promotion. I did not receive a raise or any other added benefits, only a new title. The division chair told me that that's just how it was, and I couldn't expect anything better.

I was a mother of two, pushing 40, and tired of playing

Academic Survivor. If I was so great that the division would promote me to associate, then it needed to give me a raise and a few other things, too. It was time to negotiate for real. And to do that, I needed to figure out my best alternative to negotiated agreement—my BATNA.

Start Thinking About Your BATNA

If all you do after reading this chapter is start rethinking your work situation, then you're already on your way to conceptualizing your BATNA. Having a strong BATNA means shifting the power to your hands and out of the hands of those people who force you to play *Survivor* with your colleagues. It means that—if at any point you can't reach a fair negotiated agreement with your chair or dean—you have an alternative.

Often, as you can imagine, that alternative involves leaving your current position. But not always.

Creating your BATNA is the hard part. I was lucky. My first division—with its surprise contract changes—made me paranoid about job security. My paranoia made me feel like I needed to build up outside sources of income. So I start writing books and building up a consulting business—essentially, without really planning a career for it, I started freelancing on the side. And over the course of eight years, that unplanned freelancing work started to pay off.

As I became more aware of my tenuous job security, I worked hard so my side-gigs would pay off. Then, when I got my final fake promotion, I had a strong BATNA. The strongest I could hope for, in fact: I was willing to leave the job if the division didn't meet my terms. And leaving wouldn't be a desperate move on my part. I would be leaving to do something that would make me just as happy as the job I'd been in. Leaving my job was truly a good alternative for me.

One other thing: BATNA relies on context. When you compare your academic job with your alternative career options, you might see—as I did—that your best alternative to negotiating more favorable working conditions inside academia is a strong job outside of academia. Or, you might find a new job at another campus, or in another division at your institution, and be able to use that new job as your BATNA.

My BATNA was my willingness to work as a freelance academic instead of an employee of the division that gave me the fake promotion.

But your current BATNA could be simply doing less in the job that you now hold: doing less unpaid service or holding only the minimum of office hours. All of the "adjunct heroics" (as Rebecca Schuman has put it) may need to go out the window.[4] Then you'll have time for your own work that could lead to alternative income—like writing a book or consulting on the side. You'll have time to create your BATNA now. At the very least you will decrease your anxiety because you will start building a safe place to land. After all, who knows when you might need it.

SIXTEEN

Leaving a Legacy Off the Tenure Track

For decades, psychology researchers, specifically in the psychologies of work, business, and economics, have studied the value of intrinsic motivation.[1] First observed by researchers in the 1950s, intrinsic motivation originates from internal drives to be good at things and to enjoy them.[2] It is often contrasted with extrinsic motivation, which is akin to "the carrot and the stick."

Graduate school is one long lesson in intrinsic motivation. No supervisor sits in your crappy apartment telling you to read and write, to stay late in the lab and conduct research after everyone else has left, or to prep for class after class. In other words, there is no stick. As far as carrots go, you don't get paid much (or at all) for the work you do in graduate school. You get little praise, especially in the short term. Viewed from the outside, you seem to be working, quite literally, for nothing.

All of which suggests you don't pursue a Ph.D. unless you are an intrinsically motivated person. Furthermore, students must significantly delay gratification while in graduate school, another quality of intrinsic motivation. The benefits (and negative consequences) of working (or not working) are a ways down the line—and nearly impossible to see if you are the kind of person who needs instant, external motivation to keep working.

So graduate students—in the United States, at least—are intrinsically motivated, delay gratification, and work for pennies. And here's the kicker: They do all of those things hoping for a tenure-track job that will likely never come—and, perhaps, was never meant to come.

As Kelly J. Baker pointed out in her essay "Academic Waste," graduate students earning their Ph.D.s teach undergraduates on the cheap, a system that allows universities to continue to make their budgets.[3] Baker notes, "New Ph.D. holders are not 'products' of our training, but 'byproducts' of academia. Graduate students and 'non-degreed flex workers' exist mostly to serve the university's labor demands. They generate cheap labor. Then they get replaced." If doctoral students and newly minted Ph.D.s aren't working toward the status of tenured professor, a status that seems less and less likely to ever come, then what are they working for?

Agency, Mastery, and Legacy

People who write about business psychology agree that, in our current economy, fostering intrinsic motivation in workers creates the best outcomes for businesses. Some businesses (and business gurus) call that sort of motivation "happiness." Others focus on "culture" to foster motivation. But what keeps coming up again and again across all of the business psychology books and articles I've read are three main concepts that work together as a coherent motivational theory: agency, mastery, and legacy.

What do those words mean? According to serial entrepreneur Nathaniel Koloc, writing for the *Harvard Business Review*, you can think of the three words like this:

(1) **Agency** is the "ability to choose who you work with, what projects you work on, where and when you work each day, and getting paid enough to responsibly support the lifestyle that you want."[4]

(2) **Mastery** "refers to the art of getting better and better at

skills and talents that you enjoy using, to the extent that they become intertwined with your identity."

(3) **Legacy** is your "higher purpose." It is what you want to leave behind when you leave this world. It is your bigger picture. For an academic, perhaps your legacy is a book, a documentary film, a scholarly article that means something to you, or a group of students whose lives you've touched. Only you know what you want your legacy to be.

Typically, you have to have agency in order to acquire mastery. And you have to have mastery in order to leave a legacy. The concept of legacy helps explain why contingent faculty continue to publish and present on their research—even when the work isn't paid as part of their jobs or valued in any way by their academic institutions. We are intrinsically motivated to do it. Most contingent faculty never have agency over their careers. They are assigned the same course to teach over and over, often a survey course outside of their expertise. They're often handed a pre-set syllabus and a standard textbook. There is no agency in the same introductory course, over and over, year in and year out.

And that lack of agency is a problem given how intrinsically motivated most faculty members are.

Off the Tenure Track Without Agency

Now, take a person who is so intrinsically motivated that they can earn a doctorate and stick them in a repetitive, uncreative contingent job. They likely just graduated from a program in which they wrote an entire book on an entirely new idea that they invented out of thin air. They supported that idea with an immense amount of self-directed research, research they had to conduct in order to earn the credentials required for this job in the first place.

In the new job, they teach four or five sections of the same introductory course each semester. The course uses a curriculum handed down by the department, one that is standardized across sections, so they cannot deviate from the syllabus. They have no research support. Their "colleagues" barely know their name. They are on a year-to-year contract that could be cut at any time. They have no job security.

How can we expect this kind of person to thrive in this environment? Eventually they feel caged. Then restless, and then anxious, burned out, and depressed. This life is terrible for our mental health, and worse, no one we work for cares.

The agency-mastery-legacy concept has helped me understand one of the biggest reasons why contingent faculty end up hating their jobs so much that they quit for what may seem (to people still in the academy) like boring, non-life-of-the-mind work in the private sector. Contingent faculty leave academe in search of opportunities that provide—you guessed it—agency. Then mastery. And then, hopefully, legacy.

Finding Agency Within the System

But what if you don't want to leave academe? Or can't? Can contingent faculty find agency, mastery, and legacy while working as contingent faculty? How can you make your mark?

The first thing I can tell you is this: What you want your legacy to be is a very personal decision. But the second thing I can tell you is that academics are trained to believe that their academic legacy should be one very particular thing—a monograph, a grant, a discovery. For the longest time, for example, I believed that if I didn't publish a scholarly monograph that I had failed to achieve my professional legacy.

Why did I think that? Why? I have absolutely no use for a scholarly monograph. A monograph is a book of research, published with a university press, that a professor writes for other professors to read. I have no time to write one, and it would make me no money. No job that I would ever want would care if I had one. I've thought hard about the source of my belief, and the only thing I can come up with is academic brainwashing. Such brainwashing is a powerful thing—do not underestimate its influence. Once I finally set aside the monograph goal, I felt incredibly free.

You need to be sure that what you want to leave as your legacy is what you really want—not what you think you should want, or what "real" academics want, or what you are supposed to do in order to get a tenure-track job. That's not a legacy, that's a résumé.

In many ways, working off the tenure track gives you great freedom. If you don't want to write a monograph, you don't have to. Write something else instead: a memoir, a novel, a textbook, an oral history of some fascinating historical event. Then sell it and start earning some passive income. Maybe your legacy is the students whose lives you've touched. Wonderful. Figure out a way to focus on that—try to find agency, mastery, and legacy in your teaching.

Sit down and figure out what you want to leave behind in this world. Then figure out what kind of freedom—agency—you need in order to gain the skills—mastery—to be able to produce that kind of legacy.

You already have the intrinsic motivation. You just need to point it at something, and let it fly.

SEVENTEEN

Why Attend Conferences as a Freelance Academic?

FOR A FREELANCE ACADEMIC, ATTENDING A SCHOLARLY CONFERENCE can seem like a confusing proposition.

If you're an independent scholar—that is, someone who is unaffiliated with an institution but who chooses to continue to do research in a scholarly field—attending a conference makes sense. You want to stay apprised of new research and present your own. I can understand that.

But what if you're a freelance academic, and you don't do scholarly research anymore? What if you have instead turned your research skills to generating freelance income? Scholarly conferences can seem pointless—you don't have much to offer them, and they don't seem to have much to offer you. You're no longer on the job search, so you don't need that scholarly line on your C.V. Plus, attending a conference without an institutional affiliation can feel alienating. When you have a blank space under your name rather than an institution, others at the conference struggle when they meet you, and you constantly have to justify your presence.

To make matters worse, conferences are ghastly expensive. The travel, the hotel, the conference fees, the food—you're looking at a couple thousand dollars, easy.

If you're not getting research support from an institution and you're not on the job hunt, conferences can seem like a colossal waste of time and money. And honestly, as a freelancer, what would you present on at a conference in your field? What could you possibly contribute?

The answer is: Far more than you might think.

For freelance academics who are considering attending a scholarly conference, here are some suggestions for how to overcome feelings of alienation and how to figure out what you have to contribute.

Alienation

Feelings of alienation, especially for those who have just recently left academia, might be the most difficult challenge to overcome on this front. You left the ivory tower. So why are you back on the scholarly-conference circuit? You don't have to earn tenure, so why are you presenting scholarship? What if the other conference attendees find out that you don't have an academic position? Isn't that kind of embarrassing?

Just because you don't hold an academic job doesn't mean you can't have a post within a scholarly organization. For example, I recently took a job as a mentor for a large scholarly organization; at its annual meeting the mentor program has its own gala, meet-and-greets, and other events. I'm involved in a way that isn't about teaching or research.

Kelly J. Baker, a post-academic journalist, editor, and author, wrote about her experience attending her discipline's annual meeting as the chair of a task force on contingent faculty.[1] She described how, although she wasn't in academia when she attended the conference, she had a purpose. Baker left the task force once it became apparent that her efforts weren't going to bring about change, but her efforts were still valuable. Your efforts can still be worth your time, even if you fall short of your goals.

Time and Money

It's true: Most conferences are very, very expensive. I would never suggest that you attend one for any reason if you can't afford it. Right at this moment I'm working on an accommodation for a member of a panel I'm chairing. She's disabled as well as strapped for cash. We're working out plans so that she can videochat rather than pay to travel across the country and spend money she does not have.

If you feel like a conference is going to be a waste of time and money, then trust your instincts. Don't go. Don't go just because you feel like you should. Don't go because you miss your old friends. Instead, visit them on your own time, when you can spend quality time together. Don't go because you feel like you're missing out on the zing of academia. Spending thousands of dollars on a conference isn't going to bring back the zing. It's just going to make you broke.

But there are reasons to go if you can afford it.

You can network with colleagues and clients. You can pitch a textbook to book editors. You can give a workshop on a topic, refine the workshop based on your experience, add that workshop to your résumé, and advertise similar workshops in the future, for money, because now you have experience leading such a workshop. Which leads me to my final suggestion.

What Do You Present?

Say you have decided to submit a proposal to present at the conference. What do you submit if you are no longer interested in the tenure treadmill? As a freelance academic, how can you make a conference presentation meaningful to your career outside of academia?

You can always present traditional scholarship, of course, even if tenure is not your goal. Scholarship has many benefits beyond earning tenure. Presenting scholarship can help you establish an identity as an expert in a particular field—as someone who might be hired by those outside of the field as, say, a consultant. If you present on the latest developments in a particular area of sociology, think about how your work might translate to freelance writing or consulting. Always plan a way to double-dip.

Of course, you might present your scholarship simply because you enjoy it.

Workshops

But there are other ways to share knowledge at a scholarly conference that do not involve presenting traditional scholarship per se.

Do you lead workshops as a freelancer? I do. I teach people how to pitch their work to media outlets, for example, especially former academics. The first time I gave that workshop, though, was at a scholarly conference.

So here's my last piece of advice: Suggest a workshop in your area—say, as a roundtable—at your field's conference. For example, if you lead workshops on interviewing skills as a freelancer, the conference for your learned society might be interested in having you lead a workshop for graduate students on interviewing skills as well. The same goes for workshops on résumé writing, social-media best practices, and online portfolio design. Any skill that you teach outside of academia is a skill that workers who are still in academia would likely be interested in learning.

In short, bring your freelancer skills back into the academy via a scholarly conference. You'll be surprised, too, by how many people in your learned society will be interested in what you have to teach.

EIGHTEEN

Why Am I Teaching Again?

YOU KNOW THAT JAMES BOND MOVIE WITH THE 52-YEAR-OLD SEAN Connery playing an aging Bond? The one with the tongue-in-cheek title, *Never Say Never Again*?[1] Apparently, that title referred to a statement Connery made years before, in which Connery had said he'd never, ever play Bond again. And yet there he was, up on the big screen, trying to get those nukes back from SPECTRE.

Years ago I left teaching. I'd been working in a contingent job. One of my "colleagues" even referred to my particular job status as "untenurable." (That word is apparently a thing now.) I'd had enough, so I was out the door. Goodbye. Never again.

Then, in the winter of 2016, I received an email out of the blue from the continuing education department of a local university: Would I be interested in teaching a creative-writing course for them in the spring semester?

Would I? I had no idea.

Because I do not use my gut to make professional decisions, I made a list of pros and cons. And because I'm a glass two-thirds-empty kind of person, I started with the cons.

Cons

Pay: The pay for the course would be $125 for six weeks of teaching, or $25 a course meeting. I would have to teach one 90-minute class a week, plus there would be class-preparation time. Furthermore, on the payment paperwork, there was a sentence that read, "Many instructors choose to donate their honorarium to the [continuing education] program." Let me be clear: The university that asked me to teach for it was Duke University. Duke University was asking me to donate my teaching pay to Duke University. To be honest, sometimes I feel like my job as a higher education writer is to simply record reality for other people to read, no commentary necessary.

Location: The course meeting place was located far enough away from my home to constitute an "annoying" commute.

Coffee: The building where I would be teaching did not allow food or drink, which meant that even though my class would be in the morning, I wouldn't be allowed to bring coffee to class. Up until this class, I had literally never taught a class without a coffee mug in my hand.

Pros

But there were some pros to teaching this class. It turned out that I wasn't going to be an underpaid, coffee-deprived ghoul for no reason at all.

Course content: I would be teaching a creative-writing workshop—in particular, narrative writing, my favorite. I would have complete control over my curriculum, including how many pages my students turned in each week to workshop.

Class size: I could limit the course to eight students. In fact, I could have made it smaller, but eight seemed like a good size to me. If I chose to teach the course in the future, I could have six students, or even fewer.

Class frequency: The course only met once a week, which

seemed very doable. I have never, ever taught a once-a-week course before. I wondered: What would that be like? Such a luxury! Such an extravagance!

Intangibles: The course would be a way to dip my toe into teaching a creative-writing workshop beyond the one-day workshops I'd done here and there in the past. Teaching creative writing for a university would give me credibility. The course would only be six weeks long, and let's face it, I can do anything for six weeks.

Teaching the course suddenly seemed like one of those times when exposure could actually be a good thing. And you'd better believe I took that $125 check. (Donate it? Were they serious?)

So I assigned *Bird by Bird* by Anne Lamott and headed off to teach my first "real" creative-writing workshop.[2] And it was fantastic. The students were so eager to do the work and had such great insights. I was so energized after class.

I remembered I loved teaching.

Holy crap. I love teaching.

It turns out that teaching on three campuses in two different cities while pregnant with my first child just to make a living wage wasn't able to beat my love of teaching out of me. The callous disregard of some of my so-called colleagues didn't either.

I'd really thought my love of teaching had been tortured, beaten, murdered, and buried. I'd imagined my love of teaching's tombstone: *Here lies Katie's love of teaching. It lived for 20 years, starting when she taught kiddos to swim as a teen. Killed by a four-four course load, freeway flying, and jerks.*

But no. I still love it. These eight creative writers of wildly different life experiences and skill levels reminded me why. Plus, I learned how to sneak a spill-proof coffee mug into my classroom.

But it wasn't just the students who reminded me why teaching is wonderful. Every one of the pros on my pro-con list helped, too. I had control over my course—its content, its size, its curriculum. For nearly a decade, I'd been handed a syllabus and a book and told what to teach. My own creativity could only fit in at the margins of a teaching career like that. Yes—core courses need be taught. But even in core courses, faculty can, and should, have some agency. Too many departments, however, don't trust contingent faculty. They don't allow them autonomy in their own classrooms. That's part of the problem with higher education today, and one of the reasons I left.

The best part about this course I taught was the relationship I formed with each of my students. Like you're supposed to do when you're teaching, I learned from them as much as they learned from me. They taught me about writing, about teaching writing, about all of the things that I want to be better at. I might have once said never again to teaching, but teaching again has brought me new friends, ideas, and fellow writers. And freelance academics need all the friends we can get.

PART III
Career Advice

NINETEEN

Launch Your Career Like James Bond

THIS CHAPTER IS FOR ALL OF THE ASPIRING FREELANCE ACADEMICS out there who have absolutely no idea how to get started with a new career. You might still be in the academy, but you want to start dipping your toes in the pool of new work outside of academia. Or, you might be ready to jump in headfirst. Either way, you might feel like you don't know how to become something other than an academic.

I understand, I really do. We were trained to be one thing. It's time to be something else. But that's easier said than done. Luckily, we have good role models.

I'm talking about James Bond.

Have you ever seen *Dr. No*, the very first James Bond movie?[1] It's a good movie, as the old Sean Connery Bond flicks go. But what is most remarkable about the movie, to me, is this.

After the opening sequence in which a British operative in Jamaica is assassinated, the film cuts to to an exclusive gaming club in London called Les Ambassadeurs. A man enters the club. At the door, the host stops him and asks if he is a member. The man pulls out his card and hands it over, saying he is looking for a person called James Bond.

If you were watching this movie upon its release in 1962, this moment would be the first time in cinematic history you would have ever heard that name.

The film cuts to a room in the club where woman in a red evening gown is playing a card game called "chemin-de-fer" (a version of baccarat), and she is losing against the player dealing the cards. When she calls for more chips from the bank, the voice of the unseen dealer finally speaks to her.

"I admire your courage, Miss…"

"Trench, Sylvia Trench. And I admire your luck, Mr. …"

"Bond, James Bond."

That's the first time we hear those words spoken on screen, and the first time we hear his voice.

Shortly after, for the first time, we see his face. At that moment, we hear the low, thrumming guitar score that for the past 60 years we've come to associate with James Bond.

But remember: In 1962, you'd never heard that song before. You'd never heard him introduce himself before. You didn't know who he was.

But the film writers didn't care. Watching *Dr. No*, it feels like James Bond has always existed. That he's always been wooing the Sylvia Trenches of the world at 3 a.m. at exclusive casinos in Mayfair, that he's always been sent dashing off to confront SPECTRE in Jamaica. When you watch *Dr. No* today, you wouldn't know if it were the first Bond movie or the 10th.

He's so Bond in *Dr. No* it's nearly unbearable. Because he says his name in such a way, in such a tux, in such a place that he expects you, his audience, *to already know who he is*.

Bond magically appears fully formed, like Athena springing from the head of Zeus. At the beginning of the Bond franchise, there was no birth of Bond, no origin story.

So what does *Dr. No* have to do with your freelance career?

I've coached many new writers, who are often transitioning from other careers. I get asked questions like, "I don't have a lot of clips or publications—what would I put on a website?" Or, "How do I write a social media profile when I'm basically a nobody?"

The Freelance Academic

The best advice I give is to take a page from James Bond in *Dr. No*.

You are right now, starting today, a public figure. You are, starting today, a writer, or an editor, or a consultant, or a coach. Whatever freelance career path you have chosen to take, you are, right now, already on that path. You need to simply decide that *you are what you are*, and then make sure that every public document you put out there reflects that decision.

How do you make this happen?

Let's use writing as an example. If you're looking to start a freelance writing career, you've probably written more than you think. What "counts" as writing is a bigger net than you think. What kinds of writing did you do for your academic job? Think beyond just your conference papers and journal articles. What about grants? Proposals? Slide decks? Reports for committees? Those count, too. Put a bullet point on your website about your experience with grant writing or professional writing. For example, you can make a lot of money helping businesses with their high-stakes business writing.

Second, when you create your freelance writer website, take into account all of the things that you are. Don't limit yourself to just one narrow band of interest. You will have plenty to put on your website. But the most important thing is to launch your website as though it were a website that had always been there, professional in appearance, representing you, the professional. Never say that your site is "in progress." Never have a page that says, "Under Construction." If you have an unfinished page, just leave it unpublished until it is finished. Each web page will appear online fully formed and professional (even if, in your mind, there is always more you can add. The world doesn't need to know that.)

Bond, James Bond. Dot com.

The same goes for your social media profiles—all of them. Yes, you need those, too. You are going to burst onto the public scene like Athena. You will not apologize. You will not be "beta" or "just figuring this thing out." You will be a pro from the get-go. Or, at least you will fake like you are until you are. You want to inspire confidence in other people. And you want to inspire confidence in yourself.

Look like a professional, until one day, you are a professional. And then you'll see that there's not much difference, in the end.

TWENTY

How to Start Working for Yourself

Years ago, when I quit my job as contingent faculty to work as a full-time freelancer, I had no idea what I was doing. I've been lucky, and so far, I've made a pretty good run of it. I want you to have more than luck on your side. That's one of the reasons I wrote this book.

Some of the advice I've written is meant to help you figure out your new relationship with your old career with academia. Figuring out how to separate from higher education isn't easy. Some of the advice I've written is more practical, what you will need day-to-day as you embark on your freelance academic career. Here is some advice I wish I'd had when I first started working for myself.

Getting Started

There are a few things that you need to know right out of the gate if you are going to start working for yourself. Although you might not do what I do—writing, speaking, consulting, and editing—you will likely still find some things here that will help.

The first thing you need to know is this: Your academic

training has definitely prepared you to make a living outside of academia. This fact is incontrovertible, despite anything you might have experienced in graduate school or what you might read in the popular media about how academics are useless. We're not useless. And we make good livings outside of academia all the time. The evidence supporting this claim is sound.

Here's the second thing you need to know: Your academic training has likely not prepared you to work for yourself because it has not prepared you to run a business.

What do these two things mean, together? If you want to leave academia and work in the private sector, in the public sector, or for some hybrid thereof, you are prepared to do so. Study up on how to transition and do it.

But if you want to leave academia and work for yourself, you need to learn how to work as a freelancer and also as a small business owner.

Sometimes Freelancing Isn't a Choice

Let's take a step back and appreciate that a lot of us didn't take up freelance careers because we wanted to. We did it because we had to. What is now called the "gig economy" has been forced upon workers just as contingency has been forced upon faculty in higher education. Businesses have cut back on full-time employees and replaced them with independent contractors (freelancers) who receive paychecks but no benefits. Because the businesses don't have to pay benefits, worker's compensation insurance, or FICA taxes (Medicare or Social Security), contractors save the businesses a lot of money.

A lot of workers have no choice but to turn to freelancing. They've lost their jobs, and the only way to keep working in their fields is to sell their services to various companies—often the same companies these people used to work for as employees. As independent contractors, they often make less money than they used to, and of course they have little or no job security.

Not only do freelancers have to purchase their own health insurance, but they also have to hustle for every job. Despite the positive spin that freelance-heavy companies like Uber have put on the word, "hustling" for a living isn't pleasant. Then, after a freelancer has hustled to get a job and done the work, they might get stiffed by their client, and with little recourse. According to a survey by the Freelancer's Union, half of freelancers reported getting cheated by a client in 2014.[1] Furthermore, the "average amount lost was $6,390. For the average respondent, that amount represented 13 percent of their annual income." In short, freelancers have a hard time collecting that lost money. Actual employees wouldn't have such a hard time, as the Freelancer's Union points out: "If this were to happen to a full-time employee, they would be entitled to file a wage-theft complaint with the Department of Labor." The Freelancer's Union is working on a campaign to get bills passed at the state level to protect against freelance wage theft.

In many ways, contingency is the gig economy of higher ed. So why move from one gig economy to another? If both careers—working off the tenure track and working as a freelance academic—are so similar, why not stick with what we know, contingency in academia? Because in practice, they're not so similar at all. In my job, I call the shots. I don't wait around hoping my contract is renewed. I don't have to put up with colleagues—clients—who treat me poorly.

But at the same time, the "gig" economy can be tough. Freelancing requires you to think about money in a vastly different way than you likely have in the past. You will need to pay yourself a steady paycheck, for example, even though some months you'll make less money than other months. You will need to consider incorporating or forming an LLC. These are important decisions, ones you never needed to think about when you worked for a university, and ones you don't need to think about if you choose to work for a company outside of academe. But if you are going to work for yourself, you need to think about them now.

In the early days of a freelance career, the hours will be long, and the jobs will ebb and flow. The uncertainty can be hard on your mental health, and you might believe that overwork can control the uncertainty. It can't. You will need to learn how to turn off the job at the end of the day. If you don't, you will work too many hours, day and night, developing anxiety, chronic stress, burnout, and worse. If you are able to take the risk, then the rewards are great, such as freedom to make your own schedule and to take on projects that interest you. As you establish yourself, your freedom grows even greater.

But to get these rewards, you have to take the risks. And for some people, the risks are not worth it. I understand, I really do.

If you feel that the uncertainty of a freelance career is too hard to take, then you shouldn't freelance. There is zero shame in making the choice to take on a more stable job. The jobs are out there, and you *are* prepared for them. Best of all, they are more fulfilling than you likely think they are. It's not all *Office Space* and TPS reports.[2] I promise.

I'm not here to burst any bubbles. I'm not here to say, "It's uphill both ways, whippersnapper." I'm here to mix some practicality into your planning.

Exploitation Ends Now

My first piece of advice to you is this: never (rarely) work for free.

I say "never work for free" because I'm a writer who writes for a living. I pay my mortgage with writing. I turn words into cash and buy food, diapers, and gasoline with that cash. But all of the time I'm approached by others and asked to do work for free. Sometimes, these are positive, well-meaning organizations who cannot afford to pay me. Other times, these are wealthy organizations (like universities with large endowments) who can.

As I explained in the introduction to this book, I have a theory about writing for free that guides my decision-making: There are a lot of great magazines out there that editors run for nothing. Sometimes, the magazines even lose money. These magazines publish stories that will make the world a better place. I write for magazines like that a lot. But if a magazine can afford to pay and it doesn't? That's exploitation. If it can afford to pay well, and pays poorly? Same.

Don't allow yourself to be exploited.

You can substitute a variety of verbs for "write." You know what skills you have that people pay other people for. You might be an editor. You might be a researcher. You might be a tutor, a website designer, a teacher, or a theatrical scenic designer. If you want to work for yourself, either part-time or full-time, the first step is learning how to ask people to pay you a fair wage for your work. And asking people to pay you for your work can be very hard when you are accustomed to getting a paycheck from a large institution (even a small paycheck).

In order to run your own business, you first have to value what you do. You have to value yourself. You do not edit, research, tutor, teach, or design in a way that exploits you. And you will know when you are being exploited. It doesn't feel good. You feel undervalued. It hurts inside, even just a little.

Your job, starting today, is to value what you're worth. What you're really worth. You need to do some research. Do you know how to do research? You bet you know how to do research. Find out what the going rates are in the private sector for what you do. Think about the rates that you should be charging and start charging those rates. And remember, when you set your rates, you have to add 30% to what you think a fair hourly wage will be —because from now on, you are paying all of your taxes. No employer is picking up half of your Medicare and social security. Freelancers pay it all. Plus, you have to account for all of the time that you spend quoting jobs that don't happen.

If you're a new freelancer, I can tell you right now that your hourly rate is too low. It just is. Go raise it.

Remember how you used to have a C.V.? You don't have one of those anymore. I used to have a C.V. too. When I had a C.V., and an academic career to go with it, I used to give talks for free. Conference presentations, invited lectures, lectures on my campus. Free, free, free. And then I quit my professorship. Now when people ask me to give a talk, they have to pay me to do it. They can't convince me with the "this will look great on your C.V." line. Because I no longer have a C.V. Now, I have a checking account into which I put money.

For example, soon after I started freelancing, the very university at which I used to work invited me to give a two-hour professional-development seminar to a group of faculty. I charged what I considered to be a vast amount of money. They agreed to my fee without hesitation.

Before I presented my fee proposal, I figured out how much to charge by asking around. The first thing I asked, in fact, was for "sample proposals" from the client for "prior lectures," and they sent me the proposals. I looked at the prices these other groups charged, and I charged similar prices. In other words, I educated myself about the going rate.

Full disclosure: there was a moment when I felt uncertainty. I asked myself terrible questions: Am I worth the going rate? Why me? Is this something that I'm worth being paid this much money to do? Call it self-doubt or imposter syndrome or whatever, I felt it, and I felt it hard.

And then I sent the proposal. And then, a few weeks later, I cashed the check.

Now I give talks at universities frequently. I charge plenty—I charge enough. This is my job, my livelihood. I keep a photograph of my kids on my desk because they're cute, sure. But I also do it to remind me that every hour I'm away from them on a far-flung campus must be worth it financially.

If you want to avoid being exploited and make sure you earn enough money to live on, you have to research, quote your work accurately, and bluff a little bit when you feel like maybe you aren't worth the rate you are quoting. But you are worth it. You have years of training, experience, expertise—in other words, you are an expert.

Figure out what you're worth. Quote accurately. Invoice. And get paid for your work.

TWENTY-ONE

How Can You Earn Money?

When I started my first university job after graduate school, I lasted about half a year before I started a side-gig. While working as a lecturer, I wrote and sold a nonfiction book in my area of expertise to a publisher. The book wasn't anything fancy—I just put together all my teaching materials from a course I'd created, packaged them up for a pre-existing book series the publisher already had, wrote a proposal, and sent it off.

But I still get royalties from that book today, nearly ten years later.

More importantly, writing that book helped me land my next nonfiction book project and some speaking gigs. Because I'd written a book in an area that people in my field were interested in, more jobs came my way. Pretty soon, I had three reliable income streams: my main job, my book royalties, and my speaking engagements.

I kept writing, until one day I realized I didn't need the main job anymore. The side-gigs had become my main gigs.

After leaving full-time employment, it became even more important to think about the variety of income streams that could help me earn a living. Sure, I might think of myself as a "writer," but writing encompasses so much more than book royalties. I've worked as an editor, a freelance journalist, a keynote speaker, a writing and career coach, a copywriter and designer for websites, and, of course, an author. Each one of those income streams is valuable.

When I wrote that first book, I wasn't planning on leaving my job. At the time, I was happy enough doing what I was doing. But I did feel that having more than one source of cash was a way to financial stability. A table with one leg, or even two legs, isn't as stable as a table with four. When it turned out that my contingent faculty job wasn't nearly as stable as I thought it was, I was very glad to have created the other sources of income.

So how do you get multiple income streams? Especially while working a faculty job?

What Will People Pay You For?

The first step is figuring out what you are really, really good at. What are you better at than others around you? These are your superpowers. Superpowers can be small—say you're really good at organizing stuff. Or you're great with kids; like, you're the kid-whisperer. Maybe you're great at organizing stuff and you're the kid-whisperer, in which case you need to call me, and I will hire you.

Start making a list of your superpowers. Note: now is not the time to be modest. Now is the time to be the opposite of modest. Now is the time to act like you are your mom bragging about you to her friends and making you want to hide in the closet with embarrassment.

Once you have your list of superpowers, the hard part begins—because not every superpower can be turned into money.

Although these days, it seems nearly everything can.

Right now, though, we're looking for the low-hanging, monetizable fruit. If you're the person who is super good at organizing stuff, research how to be a professional organizer and how to get started. The thing to know is this: you only need one satisfied client. After you get one satisfied client, you can and will ask for a glowing testimonial. You will put that testimonial on a Facebook business page (you will have created a Facebook business page for your business) and on your website (you will have also created one of those), and you will get more clients. You give out that client's name as a reference. Business will snowball from there.

The first client is always the hardest.

Here are some other ideas:

Create a community. Start a professional organizer blog and befriend other bloggers who write about organizing stuff. They're out there. They're always out there.

Put tips on your social media as catchy graphics and videos, with your business name and website at the bottom, so when they're shared, your business is shared, too.

Write a short ebook and give it away for free: more free advertising.

In short: become the expert that people want turn to.

Don't Blow Your Money

A side-gig does two things for you: it provides a second stream of income, which is a type of financial safety net, and it provides a creative outlet. Let's talk about each of these things.

Say your organizing business side-gig has grown successful. Your network and social media are bringing in new clients. Media outlets are paying you to write articles. You have clients all around your area who pay you good money per hour to teach them how to make their homes more livable and how to make their businesses look cool. Your small business is successful. And you did it all while holding down your faculty job, too.

Why did you do all of this extra work? To buy a bigger television? If so, please do not tell me because I will be deeply disappointed in you. The whole point of this extra work is to create financial security—remember the table with lots of legs? You did not do this extra work to be able to see the manicured stubble on Tom Brady's chin at thirty paces.

Take the extra money you earn and pay off debt—student loans, car loans, credit card loans, all of it. Once the debt is paid off, create an emergency fund. Once your emergency fund is created, start saving for retirement. Eventually, once your student and commercial debt is paid off and you have an emergency fund, *and only then*, you might be able to quit your main job.

The point is, if you blow your side-gig money on stupid stuff, you'll simply create a spending pattern that you won't be able to maintain. One day, you'll realize that your side-gig has become a second, necessary main gig, one that you can't quit. You will wear yourself out because you will be working two full-time jobs to maintain your new standard of living. In short, don't buy a bigger television.

Quitting your faculty job is not an impossible dream. It is, indeed, easier to do so if you are in a stable relationship with another adult who also has an income. It's also easier if you don't have children. But you can do it. In order to do so, you have to put your side-gig cash toward relieving financial strain rather than creating more.

In the end, choosing to be a freelance academic is about creativity. Too frequently, our creativity is stifled by the work we have to do to pay the bills, leaving us too little time to do the work we want to do to feed our souls. That's what you're aiming for. That soul-feeding work.

One day, you might find yourself so enamored with your side-gig that you want to make it your main gig. Don't dig yourself a financial hole with the extra money from your side-gig. Start creating the financial freedom that you need to one day leave your job and turn your creative, fun, entrepreneurial work into your main work.

The multiple income streams with your new main gig—

tutoring, consulting, organizing, real estate, speaking, ebook sales, literally anything people will pay you to do—all centered around your superpower, are ways to express yourself creatively.

That's how you work as a freelance academic.

TWENTY-TWO

Run Your Business Like a Business

Disclaimer: Although I am a lawyer, I am not providing legal advice. The following is for informational purposes only. You should contact your lawyer to get advice with respect to any particular issue.

WHEN I FIRST STARTED FREELANCING FOR MONEY, I ALSO HELD A full-time job at a university. Even though I didn't earn a lot of money freelancing (just a couple thousand dollars a year), I wanted to keep my two income streams separate—my freelancing income stream and my university income stream. So I created a separate business entity for my freelance income.

I started freelancing five years before the first edition of this book was published in 2019. After that, I left my university position and started freelancing full time. I've published books, freelance articles for magazine, and other writing for money. I've also earned money as a consultant, a coach, a speaker, and an editor. My work has grown and changed since I first started freelancing. And as my work has changed, I've had to get better at running my business like a business.

Sole Proprietorship

I'm now incorporated. "Pryal Consulting, Inc.," at your service. Let's talk about what lawyers typically call "small business formation." That simply means the various ways that you can organize your business legally. There are lots of ways, but I'll talk about three of them here, the ones that most freelance academics will need to consider.

There are lots of reasons to have a separate company for your freelance business. Because I have a business, I have a business checking account and credit card, and I use those accounts to pay for my business expenses, such as pens, paper, travel expenses, and website hosting (which is advertising). Keeping these expenses in a separate account makes tax time a lot easier. I don't have to mark expenses as business or not, because if I used my business account to pay for them, I know they're business expenses. And as a freelancer, I actually have a ton of little expenses that I'm glad I have a separate business card to pay for. Nothing slips through the cracks.

The great thing is that you don't have to incorporate to have a separate checking account or credit card. You only have to have a separate entity, called a sole proprietorship, with a separate Tax ID from the IRS. In fact, when a freelance academic is just starting out, a sole proprietorship is usually the best idea. A sole proprietorship is a business run by a single person (and only a single person), and the business is not registered with the state. You just decide that you are a business, and like magic, you are. Then, to get your business's Tax ID number, go the IRS website to get a tax ID (use a search engine to find the right place), and the process is very straightforward—and instantaneous. You print out the Tax ID, take it to your bank, and open a business checking account.

Another benefit to having a Tax ID is that you no longer have to give out your social security number when you do freelance work. For example, when I write for magazines—every time—I have to give them a Tax ID for payment. I would hate to hand out my social security number each time. Instead, I give out the Tax ID for my business. You can do the same. Just file for a Tax ID with the IRS. Then you set up a separate checking account to receive your payments, and you can deduct your business expenses from your business earnings without any confusion.

Limited Liability Company

However, if you decide to form a sole proprietorship, you won't get the protections that come with a limited-liability company (an LLC) or a corporation—namely, protection from liability if someone decides to sue you. Depending on your business, having this protection might be really important. Please consult your lawyer to figure out if an LLC is a better way to go for you. But don't let the need to form an LLC stop you from forming a sole proprietorship now. You can usually convert your sole proprietorship into an LLC when you are ready to do so. Get the benefits of a sole proprietorship now, then figure out if an LLC (or a corporation) are right for you.

Here's what I did. When I began earning freelance income, I formed an LLC right away. Now, forming an LLC costs money: most people have to hire a lawyer to help with the paperwork. I am a lawyer, so I did my own paperwork. There are also filing fees with your state, and in my state, those are in the hundreds of dollars, annually. Plus, you have to pay your accountant extra to do your LLC's taxes. So be sure that these extra costs are worth the protections an LLC provides.

Incorporation

After a few years, I chose to convert my LLC to a corporation, in particular, an S-Corporation. There are different kinds of corporations, depending on size and other factors. If you are a small business and want the benefits of a corporation without a lot of the hassle, an S-Corporation is your best bet. (Your lawyer can explain why.) There are two main reasons that I chose to convert my LLC to an S-Corp: I save money on my taxes because I can pay myself some of my money in a paycheck and some in dividends, which is taxed at a lower rate.

The other reason is because I can have what is called an "Individual 401(k)," or i401(k). You can only have an i401(k) if you are the only employee of your corporation. When I left my academic job, I rolled my institutional retirement plan into my new i401(k) and then continued to contribute tax-free. There are lots of investment banks that would love to help you set up your i401(k) for free. But you can only have a corporate-style retirement plan if you have a corporate-style business.

There are drawbacks to having your business structured as a corporation. Your accounting becomes far more complicated. You must pay yourself an actual paycheck and payroll taxes; I pay for accounting and payroll software to handle this for me. Remember, I'm a lawyer, and I'm good with accounting, and I still pay for that service so that I don't have to do all of that figuring. The cost is approximately fifty dollars per month. The cost for an accountant to do your corporate taxes also adds up. The point is, for as much money as you will save, you will need to figure out how much you will spend. If the savings don't outweigh the expenses and the aggravation, you shouldn't incorporate. Instead, stick with a sole proprietorship, or form an LLC if you need the liability protections.

Bookkeeping, Quoting, and Invoicing

To keep up with my accounting, I use QuickBooks. There is other bookkeeping software out there, including Xero and Freshbooks, and I've tried the others. I like QuickBooks the best. This is not an endorsement, however, because all bookkeeping software is expensive, ungainly, expensive, and also *expensive*. As soon as there is bookkeeping software that beats what exists, I will use it.

Find the one that works best for you even if you don't like it very much.

The short of it is: if you are going to run a business, you need to keep your books. You need to do real bookkeeping, what is called "double entry" bookkeeping. You don't just want a computer program that will balance your checking account, like Quicken or Mint. You want to keep your books. Research "double-entry bookkeeping" to learn more about it. Basically, if you're spending money, you want to know where that money came from—and so does the IRS. If you spend money on pens, that money has to have come from someplace. Where?

Bookkeeping software keeps track of the money coming in, and of the money going out. That's double entry, in its most basic sense: every debit (you paying someone) is tied to a credit (someone paying you). If you aren't doing double-entry bookkeeping, then you aren't bookkeeping. You will probably dislike keeping your books, but software like QuickBooks and Xero makes it less painful.

Another feature of bookkeeping software that becomes really important as you start freelancing is invoicing. At the beginning, when you are just starting out and a spreadsheet can keep your books, you can invoice with an email. Later, as you have more business, you will be glad to have invoices incorporated into your bookkeeping software. Using my software, I create invoices, send invoices, and—this is the best part—track my paid and unpaid invoices. At a glance, I can tell who owes me money.

There's plenty of work you will not love to do as a freelancer. I don't enjoy bookkeeping. I don't enjoy invoicing. I don't enjoy quoting jobs. I hate doing tax paperwork. Pretty much, I don't enjoy doing the work that I have to do that keeps my business running like a business. Whenever I'm doing any of those things, because I am me, I complain a lot. Loudly.

My husband eventually gets fed up and yells, "At least you're not grading!"

True. He listened to me moan about grading for 11 years, as I taught college writing, sometimes four sections a semester across multiple campuses across multiple cities. Nothing snaps me back to reality faster than that particular reminder.

That stuff we don't like to do—whether we're reporting to someone else or ourselves—that stuff is called "life." But at least as a freelancer, I really do get to do what I love. Some of the time—most of the time, really. My estimate is that I spend two-thirds of my professional life actually doing the work that I love, and the rest doing tasks that support the work that I love.

And if you think about it, that ratio makes total sense. How many emails with editors do I have to draft before I get a pitch just right? How many invoices do I have to send before a client finally pays me? How many proposals do I have to revise before the client accepts the project—if the client accepts it at all?

You just have to accept this one truth: Even if you are lucky enough that "what you love" is a thing that people will pay you money to do, a lot of the time you will not actually be doing that thing. And that's OK. I've been freelancing full-time for years now, and it took me a long time to realize that the invoicing, the quoting, the book-balancing are all, in their own way, great work. Because they're my work.

Honestly, I get to do that work in my pajamas, drinking my coffee from my own coffeemaker, on my own couch, with my dog. It's not that bad.

Make Your Own Colleagues

Another challenge that freelancers face that is less tangible than business formation and bookkeeping but no less daunting is this: Freelancing can be lonely. For a long time, I wondered why people would fork over good money for coworking spaces. Why pay to work with other freelancers when we already pay for places—called houses or apartments—where we can do our work for free?

Then I figured it out. Freelancers may have different motivations for going to coworking spaces, but a primary reason is for the people. The freelancers bounce ideas off of each other. They greet each other. They know that someone else knows they're alive. This community, whether you know it or not, supports your mental health. We learned about this phenomenon during the COVID-19 pandemic. Humans are social creatures, even if that human is an autistic introvert like me. Going from the bustle of campus where the barista at the coffee shop greeted you every morning to the silence of your home can shock your mental health. Loneliness can set it, and it can become something worse, like depression. Pay attention to your mental health as you make the transition out of higher education and into freelancing.

When you leave a full-time faculty job to freelance, you lose colleagues. Now, some of you might be thinking: "Awesome. My former colleagues were terrible. I would quit just to get away from being treated like garbage." But the thing is, you probably had one or two colleagues whom you liked. And even the most misanthropic person needs other people.

But what if you can't afford to pay for a coworking space? If it's people you need, you can work in libraries or coffee shops at minimal charge, but you are unlikely to find many colleagues there who do what you do.

Here's the solution I figured out, quite by accident. I created a network of colleagues, hand-picking people whom I love to bounce ideas off of. But we connect using technology. The people whom I've gathered (and whom I am still gathering) live all over the world. We organize regular monthly videochat meetings. We talk about our career challenges. We figure out how to solve problems we're facing. Usually, when I sign off of these meetings, I have ideas for new articles to pitch or business strategies to implement. They walk away with what they need. In fact, before we say goodbye, we ask each other: "Did you get what you need?" And we always schedule the next meeting before hanging up.

Everyone needs colleagues. But if you are a freelancer, you must create your own circle of colleagues, which is much, much harder—and much, much better. But please, don't try to do it alone. It's too hard. Even if you are an introvert and enjoy being alone, you need colleagues.

Decide What Jobs to Take

You will, at first, take every job that comes your way. You'll be so excited that people want to pay you to do what you do. And then, after a while, you will realize that you don't have to take every job. This is a strange moment in the life-cycle of a freelancer. It's also an empowering one. The moment you realize you call far more shots than you thought you did.

How do you decide which jobs to take?

My husband majored in physics and economics. (Can you say "major nerd"?) But having him around is great when it comes time to make rational business decisions with my work. He knows all the tricks. And let's just say that I can be a little temperamental sometimes.

Me: "This client is ridiculous! I'm quitting!"

Him: "Your client is ridiculous. You are not quitting."

And he proceeds to explain tactics for how to manage a difficult client relationship. He helps me write strategic emails that help me maintain professional boundaries. Luckily, over the years we've been married, I've managed to absorb a little of his wisdom, so I don't need his intervention 100% of the time. Just sometimes.

One of the favorite terms I've learned from him is "decision matrix." A decision matrix is a super-rational tool for making decisions, allowing you to take a bunch of variables into consideration and keep the seat of your pants out of the equation, so to speak.

When you have a decision to make that has a lot of criteria to consider (literally, a "multi-criteria decision analysis," or MCDA), you use a decision matrix to help you make your decision. I use a decision matrix to help me decide whether I should take on writing, speaking, or consulting jobs. I can't be trusted to use my instincts because when it comes to jobs, my instincts aren't trustworthy. Here's why.

Sometimes, I'm presented with work that I feel like I should take because it will help build relationships, or build my résumé, or build my reputation. I call these jobs "3-R" jobs. I feel like I should take the job because a 3-R job, even though it doesn't pay well, might (might!) lead to more work.

Sometimes, I take a job because the money is so good that I feel like I can't say no—even though I'm pretty sure I'll hate the work. After all, I quit an academic job to freelance full time. So there's always a bit of guilt lurking in the back of my mind, telling me that I'm not pulling my weight around the household with the income that I'm generating. (I call these jobs "devil's bargains.")

Sometimes I'm lucky, and I take a job that pays okay, or even well, and I actually enjoy the work, too. (These jobs land in what I call the "sweet spot.")

The thing is, as any good economist (or my spouse) will tell you, if you fill up your calendar with 3-R jobs or devil's bargains, then you have no time left for any sweet spot work that might come along. The economics term is "opportunity cost": When you choose one path, you get the gains from taking that path, but you lose the potential gains that you might have had from taking an alternative path.

Given that, as freelancers, we're working with a fixed amount of time, and given that we'd like to make some money, whenever we are presented with time and a project to fill that time with, we need to ask ourselves: "What am I working for?"

Are you working for the money? For the three Rs? Or are you in the sweet spot? You can use a simple decision matrix to help you decide, rationally, which jobs to take—rather than being driven by fears.

My fears, if you look back a few paragraphs, are easy to identify: Is my reputation strong enough? Am I pulling my weight financially?

Start by simply keeping count of the jobs you take. Just keep count. Does it feel like you're only taking soul-killing work for the money? Maybe that's because you are. Does it feel like you're taking low-paying work with little reward except to build your reputation? Maybe you're right. Does it feel like you're not having much fun with your work? Maybe that's because you aren't.

Start counting now. If you can, get some historical data too, to help you. You might be surprised by the results. Count all of your freelance work, everything you've done to earn money or to push your freelance academic career forward, even if it didn't pay.

If it turns out you're right, and you have been taking lots of jobs to feed your reputation or your bank account, and not enough to feed your soul, you now have the evidence to prove it. And you can justify saying "no" to a job in the future. You'll know that you're turning a job down because it's time for a different sort of job. You can feel super-rational while you do so, too.

As you can see, you have a lot of choices to make as you prepare to turn your freelance academic work into a business. But you don't have to do all of these things at once. You can start slow. Take one job. Create a spreadsheet to track earnings. Get a Tax ID. Do one thing a week, just one thing. Before you know it, you'll have a career on your hands, one that you love.

TWENTY-THREE

But I'm Still In Higher Ed

TAX DEDUCTIONS FOR CONTINGENT FACULTY

YOU MIGHT ENCOUNTER BARRIERS TO FREELANCING IF YOU STILL WORK in higher education. One barrier is that departments and institutions may frown on your nonacademic work because they don't want you "distracted." When I wrote my first book for money while I was contingent faculty, I was told that some members of my department were worried that my writing would "distract" me from teaching my many sections of composition—even though I was writing a textbook for the very subfield in which I taught. In freelancer terms, the university wants to be your only client. Then, some institutions have rules that bar you from holding jobs or earning income outside of the institution.

Should Contingent Faculty Be Independent Contractors?

But there are less obvious barriers as well. I interviewed "Megan" (a pseudonym), who teaches as contingent faculty at two different institutions to make ends meet.[1] Despite her multi-campus teaching, she still ends up with a "below-poverty-level adjunct salary." She pointed out "one humongous issue" that "has to do with how institutions hire adjuncts and how [adjuncts] are taxed." Megan argues that contingent faculty "should be hired as regular freelancers, so that we can actually deduct expenses, such as partial use of home as office, since we are never given an individual office."

Her exasperation is plain in her tone: "It is completely absurd that we are taxed like regular employees, but have absolutely no benefits, and then we cannot even deduct the costs of our own work. This is really too much."

It's true that freelancers typically lack the security of regular employment, but they have the benefit of deducting their work expenses. Pens, paper, laptops, printers, home office space: the things that contingent faculty use to do our jobs.

When you freelance outside the academy, you are doing external work that is not taxed like your work at your institution. The income from that external work is sometimes called "1099 income," and you would deduct your freelance expenses against that income. However, finding the time to pursue 1099 income while teaching as contingent faculty full-time on two campuses can be next to impossible. Most contingent faculty are just too busy.

Would a better solution be to classify contingent faculty as independent contractors rather than as employees? Is such a thing even possible?

What the IRS Says

To answer my questions, I interviewed tax law professor at the University of North Carolina School of Law, Kathleen DeLaney Thomas.[2] My first question: Under tax law, can contingent faculty be classified as 1099 employees?

That's unlikely, according to Thomas: "The IRS has taken the position in most cases that adjunct professors are employees," she said, "and courts have generally agreed." That classification really isn't up to the employer. "In fact," Thomas said, "it can be more expensive for the employer to hire an employee because the employer is then responsible for FICA taxes, federal and state unemployment, and possibly worker's comp" whereas employers "can avoid payroll taxes and withholding obligations for independent contractors, who have to pay self-employment taxes on their own."

Because of the benefits that would accrue if they could classify adjuncts as 1099 workers, Thomas explained, "My sense is that schools are classifying their adjuncts as employees to avoid challenge by the IRS."

But what about the classic "freeway flier"—the contingent faculty member who teaches on multiple campuses and lacks almost any institutional support? While "the 'freeway flier' is a sympathetic case," Thomas said, "unfortunately for those professors, the precedent for independent contractor status is not good."

The problem has to do with how courts determine who is an independent contractor and who is an employee. "The determination," Thomas said, "is generally based on a facts-and-circumstances test, where courts consider a number of factors like how much control the employer exercises, which party invests in work facilities, which party bears the risk of profit or loss, and whether the work is part of the employer's regular business." Most of the factors in that test weigh on the side of the contingent faculty being an employee.

She pointed to a United States Tax Court decision, *Schramm v. Commissioner*,[3] that "held that an adjunct college professor teaching online courses was an employee, notwithstanding the fact that the professor provided his own computer and Internet connection and had no office at the school." How could that be the case? "Among the factors pointing toward employee status," Thomas said, "were that the school determined the class schedule, managed registration of students, provided the web interface for the class, and bore all risk of profit and loss, along with the fact that the courses taught were part of the school's primary business." Those factors, she said, "are likely to apply to most adjunct professors, even those that work at multiple schools."

In the end—however much contingent faculty may feel like they aren't treated as employees—in the eyes of the IRS, they will be for the foreseeable future. Our university teaching will not count as freelance work, which means we won't be able to deduct any expenses related to that work.

I'm sorry to be the bearer of that bad news, but Megan's question was an important one. Those of us who embrace the freelancer ethos need to understand the structural limitations on our freelancing work.

Tax Deductions Are Still Possible

But we can still find freelancing work outside of our institutions. The university is, after all, just another client. So you want to deduct your laptop, pens, printer, paper, and all of your other purchases on your taxes? Great—you can, so long as you deduct it from money earned through your freelancing work. If you can, turn down that fourth or fifth adjunct course, and use that time to earn money through freelance work instead. Educate yourself about IRS rules. It's not that complicated, I promise, and there are great resources out there. The Freelancers Union has lots of them online.

I know that everything I've recommended requires risk-taking on your part. I've taken those risks, too, and they're scary. One day, I walked away from relatively secure employment—as secure as a contingent faculty member can get, really. I walked away because the working conditions were just too hard on my mental health. That was one of the scariest days of my life, and my depression and anxiety were in full control of my brain because I'd been living under chronic stress for years. You don't just automatically snap out of chronic stress when you walk away from a job. It takes weeks or months for your body to recalibrate. So I worried about money, finding work, and so much more. The risks felt even bigger than they were. I felt like we were going to go broke. (We weren't.)

But then a magical thing happened. Although the first year was a little lean, I had planned well. Gradually, my mental health improved, and around that same time, I started making more money more reliably. I had all of this time to try new things, and some of those things started to pan out. I realized that no one knows how to rustle up work like a person who taught first-year writing on multiple campuses in multiple cities while pregnant. I just needed to redirect that energy in a way that benefited a career that I controlled, rather than benefiting institutions that didn't care about me at all. Oh, and I needed to take it easier on myself, too.

You can do it too. You can take all of your energy and drive and succeed in whatever path you choose, whether that path is remaining in academia and freelancing on the side, working part-time in academia and part-time freelancing, or leaving academia completely like I did and finding an entirely new career that makes you happier, healthier, and more successful—however you define success.

TWENTY-FOUR

It's Not Personal. It's Strictly Business

NETWORKING ADVICE

Recently, I was talking with a fellow freelance academic about some of the challenges we've faced making the transition out of academia and into freelancing. We both pointed to a similar challenge: A lot of the work that we were expected to do for free in the academy is work that we charge money for now.

That may not sound like a challenge at first mention. Actually, if you are still in the academy, the notion of getting paid actual money for some of the "bonus work" that you do might sound outstanding. Indeed, as my friend and I agreed, freelance academics can sometimes manage to pay the bills when we are able to effectively charge money for our hard work as editors, writing coaches, and the like.

But getting paid as a freelancer for work that you used to do for free as a faculty member can get tricky.

Here's an example. When I was in the academy, I often edited articles for colleagues and helped them with their other writing projects. I'm a good editor. In fact, I'm a trained editor who worked at newspapers and PR departments back before graduate school. I have a master's degree in nonfiction writing in addition to my doctorate. I coached people through writing challenges for work before entering the academy. When I became a faculty member, doing the same editing work for colleagues came naturally to me.

What I began to notice, however, was that those colleagues rarely returned the favor. Perhaps they felt that they didn't have the writing chops to assist me with my work. Or perhaps they just didn't view my research and writing as important. I was contingent faculty, after all, and my research didn't count toward promotion and retention. Helping me with my writing just wasn't as urgent.

Whatever the reason, I did a lot of uncompensated work as a writing coach and editor when I was in the academy. I considered it service to my departments. Then I left the academy, and one of my income streams became writing coaching and editing—not just for academics, but for novelists, journalists, and more. This time, when academic colleagues came to me for the same kind of writing help that I used to give them for free, I asked them to pay me for my time and expertise. Some of them dipped into their research funds and did so.

Some of them got mad.

So what gives? If you're a freelancer and former academic, a lot of these business challenges arise because the relationships you have—or used to have—are with people still in the academy. Some of them, frankly, do not want to pay you for services you used to provide them for free. How do you manage the emotions of your former colleagues? How do you handle friends (or "friends") who come to you for help and want that help for free? How can you tell if someone is a friend or a client?

Here are some rules of thumb to keep in mind when embarking on a freelance academic career, rules that will help you transition your relationships as you transition your career out of the academy. First, remember what Michael Corleone said to his brother in *The Godfather*: "It's not personal, Sonny. It's strictly business."[1]

Business Etiquette Is Crucial

A lot of the confusion in business relationships between people who are also friends arises because the participants don't practice proper business etiquette. Instead, they think that, because they are friends, they can ignore business etiquette. But actually, the opposite is true. When friends do business together, business etiquette becomes even more important.

Here are two different examples that show why this is true.

Example 1: I have friends who own a magazine. I always pay for my subscription. But they have other friends who expect free subscriptions simply because they know the magazine's publishers. The thing is, my publisher-friends make a living—feed their children—from this magazine. Why would any so-called friend pass up the chance to pay them for their hard work? Asking for a free subscription is not friendship, it's mooching. And moochers, dear readers, are the worst.

Example 2: I have friends who own a restaurant. I love to eat there. I buy delicious food and wine, and I always tip the waitstaff ridiculously well. I never, ever mention that I'm friends with the owners. Name-dropping the owners of a restaurant is not only annoying to everyone who works in the restaurant, but it is pretentious, too. Ugh. But the owners have other so-called friends who come in to eat and expect special treatment—free drinks, free desserts, all sorts of things. They wave their "friendship" around like a discount coupon, mooching right and left.

In order to preserve your friendship with someone you would also like to do business with, you must do your utmost to behave in a professional manner. If you are the client, then pay for your friend's services in full, in a timely fashion. That's it. Period. You don't get a discount unless your friend offers one. Don't even ask. If you ask, you are a moocher. Worse, you risk losing your friend forever.

If you are the freelancer selling your services, you also must behave with proper business etiquette. Here's what that means:

The Freelance Academic

Don't get aggravated with your friend/client over personal issues. Keep your personal knowledge of your client out of your business relationship. I know from experience that sometimes, keeping things professional can be really hard. Sometimes you want to get annoyed with your client. Sometimes you feel like it would be easier to take things personally. But trust me, once you realize that "it's strictly business," a weight lifts from your shoulders.

Michael Corleone was right. (About this at least—he's not a model dude otherwise.)

Here's an example from my own freelance academic career: I had a client who paid me monthly with a personal check. (Others usually pay me via credit card or PayPal.) Often, she was late with her payments, but I overlooked that behavior, attributing it to her slightly scatterbrained nature. Then one month, she bounced a check. I had literally never had a client bounce a check before. Not only did I not have my fee from her that month, but the bank also charged a bounced check fee. Depending on your bank, those run around twenty dollars. (These fees are called "nonsufficient funds fees" or NSF fees.) I was super pissed off when the check bounced. But I talked with some other small business owners and got some good advice. "It's just business, Katie," they said. "Put an NSF policy on your invoices from now on." What about the client? "Charge her a fee and send the invoice again."

So I did. And the client paid it, not only with no questions asked, but gratefully and apologetically. And I felt an immense relief. I didn't need to feel strong emotions. I just needed to run my business. The next time she bounced a check (yes, it happened again), I didn't even flinch. I just did the paperwork. Bounced checks, like clients, are part of a freelancer's life. She's not a bad person. She's just a client who makes mistakes—ones that I don't take personally—because they're not personal.

Who Is a Friend?

But how do you know who is a client in the first place? What about those friends who think the work you do for them should be free? The rule is simple:

A friend can return a favor. A client's favor is money.

This rule is hard to follow when you first leave the academy. At first, you don't know what favors you need. You don't know anything, let alone what to charge your clients. You hardly know what kind of paper you need for your printer. But as you go along, you start to figure out how to distinguish clients from friends. Friends do things for one another. Clients take the things you do for them, and they give you money in return.

The transactions are different.

But notice—and notice well—that they are both transactions. Friends still make a trade. They just trade favors. My friends and I refer to these favors as "chits." (A chit, by the dictionary, refers to a voucher that records a sum owed to someone else.)

Discerning a friend from a client can be tricky. Other writers send me emails asking to "pick my brain" about my career path and my writing. I tend to err on the side of not-client, so I end up with a lot of hours spent doing writing and career coaching for free, for people who have no intention of doing anything for me in return. They either don't want to—because they don't understand the system of chits—or they can't—because they don't have the connections or know-how to provide anything in return.

I actually believe that most, if not all, people in the situation I just described can indeed provide something in return. The problem is that many people don't understand chits. You, dear reader, are going to understand chits.

Here's how chits work: if you ask someone to do you a professional favor, offer to do them something in return. Think of something specific that you might be able to do for them, like this: "Thank you for your time today. I'm an excellent copyeditor. If you ever need copyediting in the future, I'll be happy to copyedit an article for you." The other person might not realize that you have that expertise. The best thing about offering a valuable chit in return is that you make yourself a valuable part of the person's network—rather than a moocher.

It follows, too, that if you are the person providing a service, you can tell your friend what you would like in return as your chit. You can't expect someone to read your mind and know what you need. Here's how I recently handled this very situation. I met a new freelancer for the first time just a couple of a weeks ago. Prior to our meeting, we knew each other casually, mostly from social media. She initiated the meeting. Just before our meeting, I scoped out her website and studied her expertise. Now, I already knew why she wanted to talk to me because she'd told me in an email—I knew what she was getting from me. What could she give me in return? At the beginning of our meeting, I told her exactly what I wanted as my chit, something that I knew she would be happy to give to me in return. Suddenly, our relationship was in professional balance.

Because that's the thing about chits. When you are able to return a favor to someone who has helped you, you feel good about yourself. You feel that you aren't a mooch. You feel like you're pulling your professional weight, which is a great feeling. By handing my new friend the opportunity to give me something in return in the future, I put us on equal footing. I did it on purpose because I wanted to be friends with this person. I wanted her to know that I respect her professionally.

But not every client is a friend. If you're still in the academy, and we weren't friends before I left, and you ask me to edit your new article, I will ask you to pay me for my time and expertise. We weren't friends then, and we aren't friends now. Furthermore, I don't have a service requirement to meet. Hell, as a contingent faculty member, I never did. I was just afraid of getting fired, so I did all I could to ingratiate myself.

These days I'm a freelancer with whom you are asking to consult because you feel like you need extra help. That's great.

Furthermore, you are asking me to do a job that is squarely within the defined parameters of the work I get paid to do. You only have to read my website to know that. Indeed, you probably already know that. You already know that I'm a great editor because you likely have had me edit your stuff before, back when we were colleagues. But things are different now. Now I edit for money. That might seem crazy to you because you still draw a salary from a university. But it's true. I make a living helping academics and other writers make their writing better. And my time is valuable.

It's not personal. It's strictly business.

TWENTY-FIVE

Three Stories from Freelance Academics

I'VE SPENT THE LAST FEW CHAPTERS TALKING ABOUT HOW I DO THINGS as a freelance academic. But what about others? I thought I'd add a few more voices to the mix. How are others faring after leaving the academy? Are they succeeding?

For answers, I reached out to three freelance academics who are doing just that. Heidi Scott Giusto, Greer McPhaden, and Jennifer Polk are all post-academics who have successfully transitioned into freelance work. Their stories can help you, directly or indirectly, succeed as freelance academics. Heidi, Greer, and Jennifer are from different places (Durham, NC; New York, NY; and Toronto, Canada). They have had different training and different paths through the academy. But they share a common quality: They've all made their way as self-employed freelancers and entrepreneurs.

I posed the same three questions to each of them: What was the hardest thing for you when you transitioned out of the academy? What's the most important gift you've given yourself? What advice do you have for new freelance academics? Here's what they had to say.

Freelance Academic No. 1: Heidi Scott Giusto

About Heidi: A white woman living in Raleigh, NC
Degree: Ph.D. in history
Former life: Graduate student, writing center tutor at a large university
Currently: Consultant, writer, editor, and owner of Career Path Writing Solutions (careerpathwritingsolutions.com)

What was the hardest thing for you when you transitioned out of the academy?

Heidi writes, "My immediate transition was not that difficult because I had been preparing for quite some time." But, she notes, "As my business has grown—I'm approaching the two-year mark for running Career Path Writing Solutions—I've become aware of my lack of formal business training." In retrospect, she says, "If I could do it all over again, I would have researched whether I could have taken some business courses while I was [at my former institution]."

What has been the most important gift you've given yourself as you've made your way as a freelancer?

Choosing a fulfilling career was Heidi's gift to herself. She enjoys "feeling like I'm making a difference in people's lives in a direct way. Because I help with a variety of high-stakes documents ranging from résumés, cover letters, and LinkedIn profiles, to graduate school personal statements to website content to college applications, I get to help people at various, key moments of their lives." Heidi's words show how much she loves what she does: "To ease a person's anxiety level and burden when undergoing such stressful moments is gratifying. My job is very fulfilling."

The Freelance Academic

What advice do you have for new freelance academics?

"First, take time to brainstorm and determine your niche," she said. "I recommend choosing a field or area you already enjoy." Second, "Start getting experience and building your network outside of academia sooner rather than later. It takes a while to build a strong referral network, but once that takes shape, business snowballs." Third, and on a related note, "Don't let fear paralyze you. People self-impose limitations that lead to inaction because they fear failure, so don't let any insecurities weigh you down." In short: Figure out your strengths, build your network right away, and believe in yourself.

Freelance Academic No. 2: Greer McPhaden

About Greer: A Black woman living in New York, NY
Degree: M.B.A.
Former life: Director of research operations at a university medical center
Currently: Consultant, writer, and owner at 272 Words (272words.net).

What was the hardest thing for you when you transitioned out of the academy?

Not having anyone to talk to about her choice to leave academia and start a business was the hardest thing, Greer said. "Academics and even academic administrators aren't entrepreneurs," she told me. "Provided you've chosen the right field of study, [academia is] not a risky path. Risk makes people uncomfortable." Many of her colleagues found it hard to relate to her risky choice to leave the academy. But she understood why: "Just deciding to start a company...is a very risky thing when you have a whole academic path in front of you. It's hard for people to be supportive of your made-up job when you've had a steady job at a top university for over a decade."

> What has been the most important gift you've given yourself as you've made your way as a freelancer?

Becoming a freelance entrepreneur in the first place—"realizing that I'm okay with this"—was her greatest gift to herself. "I didn't know I was this person," she said. "I like order, and I assumed that meant I needed to know where I'm going to be, and what I'm going to be doing, 12 months from now." And yet, she told me, "it's been over 18 months and I'm still alive. I live in my same apartment. I'm not living on ramen noodles. And most people think I look more relaxed. It took about a year to come to this conclusion, but now that I have, I'm going with it."

> What advice do you have for new freelance academics?

Like Heidi, Greer was very clear with her advice: "Get a coach, a mastermind group, or a meet-up group. If you are the only person in your head every day, you will go crazy." She learned first-hand from her own experience of feeling isolated: "You—and most of the people you know—only know one way of living and working. You will compare everything to that"; that is, to academia. Instead, "you need someone who will cheer you on and tell you that what you are going through is normal."

Freelance Academic No. 3: Jennifer Polk

About Jennifer: A white woman living in Toronto, Canada
Degree: Ph.D. in history
Former life: Graduate student, frustrated freelance researcher, and virtual assistant
Currently: Coach, speaker, consultant, and owner at From Ph.D. to Life (fromphdtolife.com).

The Freelance Academic

What was the hardest thing for you when you transitioned out of the academy?

Jennifer felt "very alone" when she first left the academy. "Everyone I knew who shared my educational background was either working as a professor or trying hard to do so." She added, "Even my freelance clients were convinced I'd end up a professor." And she didn't feel like she had anyone to turn to for help: "No one had any other ideas for me, not really." So she hired someone to help her and reached out to others: "It was only after I hired a career coach and started to do informational interviews with fellow Ph.D.'s who'd moved on to other careers—and then getting on Twitter and seeking out people with my same interests and concerns—that I felt better able to take positive steps forward."

What has been the most important gift you've given yourself as you've made your way as a freelancer?

"Patience," Jennifer told me. Although she says she has to be careful to guard against "complacency," Jennifer noted that "patience more often is about giving myself the time and space and compassion to follow my own path, whatever it is."

What advice do you have for new freelance academics?

First, Jennifer urges us to consider identity a malleable thing: "Your degree or research area or award-winning syllabi are not who you are. Who you are isn't tied to any one job that you do, such as working as a professor." She deliberately used the phrase "working as" rather than "being a" professor—because "language matters." Second, Jennifer told me, "If you're feeling uncertain or unmoored as I once did (and still do on occasion!), connect with your roots…that is, your priorities, goals, values, and character strengths—and then act in accordance with them."

All three of these freelance academics took different paths and now do very different work. But their stories share common threads, and common advice: Find your community. Don't be afraid to ask for help. Figure out what you're good at and what you love, and then do it. Believe in yourself.

PART IV
Writing for the Public

TWENTY-SIX

So You Want to Be a Freelance Writer

A LOT OF FREELANCE ACADEMICS, ESPECIALLY THOSE IN THE humanities and social sciences, want to make at least some of their money from freelance writing. But the nuts-and-bolts of how to do so can be more complicated than people think when they first get started.

When I quit my full-time academic job to write for a living, the first thing I did was take an online course on how to pitch and submit freelance articles, and it changed my life. I knew that I knew nothing about this work. I needed to learn how to write freelance pieces that pay actual money, how to properly pitch articles, and how to interact with editors. But the course taught me so much more than these things.

As I worked to make a career as a freelance writer, I came to learn that you can't actually feed your family on the bagels that online venues pay for your pieces. Information on how much (and how little) magazines pay freelance writers is crowd-sourced. Search for it online.

Therefore, one particularly valuable component of the course I took consisted of interviews with freelance writers in which they described how they actually made a living. The interviewees, in an anonymous fashion, listed where their money came from each month. Their lists weren't sexy, but they were real, and they made me feel so much better about my chances of actually making it. The interviewees also provided really practical tips about how to make your money work as a freelance writer, when pay might be downright unpredictable.

So I'm here to tell you that you can make a living as a writer, but you (might) have to let go of some notions of what "making a living as a writer" means.

Where Does the Money Come From?

Just like those freelance writers did in that course I took all those years ago, I'm going to tell you where my money comes from as of 2024:

I publish nearly twenty pieces in magazines each year. Twelve of these essays are solely for the exposure because the pay is so little—something that I do not recommend usually—because I write for a huge platform. The other four to six pieces I write for paying magazines, and I earn about $3,000 per year writing those. All of these articles do more labor for me than just earning money. They help sell books and get me speaking gigs. When I first started out, I wrote four different columns in magazines and published three to five freelance articles a month. That work got me started, and it was thrilling. Now that my career has matured, my "freelance" writing is more books and less magazines.

I have published six textbooks. These textbooks earn me respectable royalties every year, especially one, which earns me a whole lot. It is not unusual that one book outearns the rest of your books by a lot like this. Although royalties fluctuate, averaged over the past five years I earn about $65,000 a year from textbooks. I got started writing textbooks because I wrote one, and that one led to another, and another, and another, until I made enough to leave my contingent job. I call this the "Kristin Hannah Effect." Kristin Hannah published twenty or so books before she published *The Nightingale*. And then once she published that huge bestseller, all of her other books sold too. But nothing sold like *The Nightingale*. The moral of that story is to just keep writing. However, I am no longer writing textbooks.

I have published, including this book, four trade nonfiction books, and I have a fifth on the way. "Trade" nonfiction means books for a general audience. These books are reviewed well, but they aren't huge sellers. My biggest sales happen when universities adopt them for courses or for campus reading groups. Their biggest help for me is when they encourage groups to hire me for speaking gigs. I probably earn $4,000 a year from trade nonfiction. Although, per the Kristen Hannah effect, because I write a trade nonfiction book every year or two, that amount will grow. You have to write books to sell books.

I have published four full-length novels, and I have more on the way. The income from these is negligible right now because I am not marketing them or publishing new novels. When I tell people this fact, they gasp. "But you're an Amazon bestseller!" or "Why do it then?" Answer to the first question: being a "bestseller" is a funny thing these days—it's true that thousands and thousands of people have my book now, and that's important to me. But selling lots of copies doesn't translate into lots of money, strangely enough. Answer to the second question: I write novels because I love it. If someone handed me two thousand dollars and said, "Go write a novel," that would be worth it to me. See also: The Kristin Hannah effect.

Lastly, and importantly, I'm a keynote speaker, which is closely tied to my writing. Organizations bring me in to speak as a direct result of my writing. My speaker's bureau represents authors. They negotiate book sales as part of my speaking gigs. My speaking is my second-highest earner after my textbooks, around $30,000 a year. But it wouldn't exist without my books and freelance writing. The writing is how my clients find me.

How much of what I just described is freelance writing for magazines? Not a lot. Writing for magazines is a lot of work. But it is very visible work, especially when a piece goes semi-viral on social media. But when it comes to how much money they earn me, freelance journalism is a terrible way to make a living. But it is a good way to earn some money as part of your overall career, and it can lead to other work, like speaking jobs and book deals.

There is a word for the type of career I have: a "portfolio career." The term comes from Liz Koblyk, former higher ed faculty turned strategic planning entrepreneur: "A concept I come back to, time and again, is that there is no one right career. There is not one lone job title that's the key to meaningful work for you. You have multiple skills, interests, values and quirks that you could (and likely will) bring to bear in multiple lines of work."[1] And that's okay.

Going forward, I see my work this way: First, I will continue to publish articles in magazines because I enjoy the quick turnaround and getting new ideas out to people quickly. Second, although I am done writing textbooks, I will continue to work new editions when required. Third, I will continue to write trade nonfiction and novels because that is writing that I love and drives my speaking career forward.

I am an author. I am a freelance writer. I am speaker. These identities are not mutually exclusive. In fact, the opposite is true. They are symbiotic.

The Transition from Academic Writer to Freelance Writer

We all have different talents that we can share with the world. The first step is figuring out what yours are—and what yours are not. For example, I am a terrible, horrible, no good, and very bad proofreader, and I do not enjoy copyediting. When I used to do developmental editing for money, in my proposals, I specifically stated that the services I would be providing do not include proofreading or copyediting. But those things might be your jam. Start networking. Get proofreading and copyediting work.

Say you are excellent at assessing websites. Like, you go to a website and in five seconds you can tell not only why it is terrible but how it could be better. The fonts make your eyes bleed. The words are a mess. You have some sort of mastery of web design and content that is a gift. Guess what? You are now a freelance writer who specializes in web content. Go figure out how freelance web content writers and designers get work.

Go make a living as a freelance writer.

But what if you want to be a freelance journalist? You want to write 1400 words for $150 on a 48-hour deadline? Okay, let's talk about that.

In my first novel, *Entanglement*, the hero (Timmy) and heroine (Greta) end up working together in a theatrical lighting company owned by the hero, called Pacific Production Lighting.[2] Pac Lighting owns hundreds of stage lights, thousands of meters of cable, multiple lighting control boards, and more. When Greta, the heroine, first enters Pac Lighting's warehouse, she's awestruck by the huge space and the huge amount of strange gear.

At readings, audience members often asked me how on earth I know so much about such a unique business. Did I just do a lot of research? The answer: Sort of. My husband owns a company very similar to Timmy's. To create Timmy's company, I just used a preexisting database in my head (and in my husband's head), put the company on the West Coast instead the East Coast, and voilà, Pac Lighting was born. That's how you use your expertise in your writing. (Although researching new stuff is really fun, too.)

If you're an author, you already know about using your expertise in your writing. If you're an academic researcher, you already know something about having an area of expertise and writing about it.

Both of those kinds of writing—writing novels and writing academic journal articles—take a long time. To write freelance articles for online venues, you need to consider your skills as a researcher and writer, and then speed them up. Way, way up. When you're talking about freelance journalism, you're talking about zippy work, and I mean fast-paced, dizzying work. The feedback, and the money, come quickly.

You're going to need to let go of some of those things that made you a good academic writer: the desire to research until you knew everything there is to know—you just won't have time for that anymore. The desire to avoid pissing anyone off in your field. You're going to piss off a lot of people, now. The desire to hedge, and then to hedge your hedges. Now, you're going to have to plant your flag on a hill and defend it.

You're going to need to know your beats. You're going to need connections with editors who get you, who get your skills, and who get your quirks. You're going to need to know how to write a pitch. You're going to need to make good friends with deadlines.

Here are some ideas to get you started.

Turn Your Expertise into Your Beats

I'm going to go out on a skinny limb and guess that, as an academic, you have areas that you are super knowledgeable about. You have vast amounts of information in your brain about niche subjects. That's because everyone has something that they are really geeky about. And also because that's what it means to be an academic. If you're lucky, you have more than one area of expertise. And if you're even luckier, you have a hobby, too, that you know a lot about. These areas are about to become your beats.

In journalism, a "beat" is an area that you have in-depth expertise in. An editor might ask you, "What are your beats?" And, if you were me, you'd reply, "Higher ed, disability, mental health, sexual assault, and first amendment issues." I didn't start out with all of those beats. They grew as I worked more.

So how did I start? I started by writing a column on mental health and disability in higher education for an arm of *The Chronicle of Higher Education*. The more I wrote this column, the more I learned about the subject. The more of an expert I became.

But I was already an expert before I started because disability studies was one of my research areas. I took my main area of research, added a whopping dose of personal experience, and a column was born.

So, to find your beats, start by making a list of the things that you are an expert in. What are your areas of research, and how might these translate to something you can write about today? Here are some questions to get you started: (1) What are you an expert in? (2) What do you do for fun? (3) What could you write about as an expert with little extra work on your part? You might expand your beats with more research as you go, but as you begin, you want to find your easiest way in.

As you jot down your areas of expertise, start adding possible topics that you might want to write about. These are areas that you might have researched recently to solve a problem in your own life, or areas that you wish you knew more about. Tie your areas of expertise to current events.

After you make your list of expertise and possible topics, you need to figure out who would be interested in reading what you have to say about these areas. What magazines run pieces about your topics? What's trending, right now? Are any of your ideas "evergreen"—journalism-speak for always on trend? Or are some of them more urgent than others—are they "timely"? You need to find your targets, and then pitch them your timely pitches "pegged" to the current event.

Find Your Targets

When you were working as an academic, what venues did you like to read? I'm talking about magazines that are online, niche, interesting—and where you found stories that seemed like stories you thought you might be able to write. That's where you should be pitching.

Think about the stories you want to write, read the magazines where you think you might see them in print, and then make a list. I use a spreadsheet software for this list because I also keep track of editors' names and their email addresses. But note:

editorial staff change frequently, so always double-check before you send a pitch. I also keep track of the last time I pitched or published a story with that publication. But a simple list will do to get you started.

Don't forget to look at trade magazines. These pay well, by the way. A general rule of thumb: the less high profile a venue is, the more it pays freelancers. Trade magazines for medical supply devices pay really, really well. But no one you want to see your byline will see it. Your piece will never trend on social media. But if you want to make a living as a writer, make friends with trade magazines. Do you keep a backyard chicken coop? If you recently had to help your heirloom chickens through some health problems with the aid of your veterinarian, you could pitch a story to a veterinary or farming trade magazine.

Then there are company websites. You could look for in-house blogger or copywriter jobs. Mostly, I get my professional writing jobs through networking, and through closed Facebook groups for people who do the work I do. You need to let people know what you are an expert in. That means you need a website, and you need to pitch stories.

Once you've compiled your list of targets to go with your areas of expertise, it's time for the next step.

Find Your Angles

An "angle" is a new thing to say about something old. "Higher education exploits adjuncts" is old news. A new angle would be something like, "Some universities are asking adjuncts to work for free, taking exploitation to new lows." This is a real thing, by the way. Check out higher education critic John Warner's piece, "Volunteer Faculty: The Death Knell for Public Higher Ed."[3]

As a freelance writer, your job is to find new things to say about your areas of expertise and to pitch those things as stories to editors. The only way to know what other people are already saying is to read what's out there. Once you've read what's out there, you can figure out new things to say—that is, new angles.

After you've done your research in an area, start brainstorming story ideas. Really let your brain go free. Write down every crazy idea for a story that comes to your head. You want to have ten so you can pick the best one.

But you might end up publishing all ten, so don't lose track of them.

After all, if you sell one story, then write it, and then publish it (in a matter of days—it's usually a matter of days), you can turn around and sell an updated version of the story, with new information, building on that first story, the following week. Writing on the same topic isn't wrong—it's called "having a beat." In fact, you put that earlier publication in your pitch (that's called a "clip") to show that you know what you're doing, and editors are more likely to hire you to write about the subject again.

If you play this right, you will be in possession of a burgeoning freelance journalism career: You will have identified your beats. You will have identified your targets—the places where you want to publish the pieces you write. You will have come up with angles on topics that you can pitch. After you publish a piece, you'll have your first clip.

You'll want to make sure that you are not bringing too much academic language into your journalism writing, but a good friend or two can help with that—before you send out your first piece, get some brutal editorial help from friendly readers. You will need to learn how to pitch articles and interact professionally with editors, which I discuss in later chapters.

Writing an academic monograph takes years and makes you little money. Writing academic journal articles takes months, sometimes years and makes you no money. Writing short freelance pieces for online venues is fast work, and a great way to balance out longer projects such as trade nonfiction or textbooks, both of which make you money.

Working as a freelance writer is fun, hard, satisfying, hard, creative, and hard. But if it is what you want to do, then you can do it.

TWENTY-SEVEN

Ten Questions Every Academic Should Ask Before Writing for the Public

HIGHER ED FACULTY ARE HAVING AN ONGOING CONVERSATION ABOUT how much to engage with the popular audiences. Writing for the public is a great way for a freelance academic to engage beyond their institution.

As a longtime freelance writer and editor, I'm writing this chapter for anyone in or adjacent to higher ed looking to connect with readers beyond the ivory tower. Here are ten questions that every former or current academic should ask *before* writing for the public.

No. 1: Who is my public?

Chances are, you already write for "a public." If you are a faculty member, you might write articles for journals or give talks at conferences. If you are an administrator, you might write reports for various stakeholders, including the general public. If you are a graduate student, you might already be presenting at conferences or publishing in journals.

But it's time to expand your definition of "public" and to understand who that audience might be. Then you must make sure you know how to best write for your new readers. For now, consider "the public" to mean this: educated people who read popular magazines and websites that you also like to read. What venues do you turn to for your daily commentary on world events, large and small? The readers of those venues compose your public audience.

No. 2: Why do I want to do this?

Some people start writing for popular publications because they think they'll earn money. Some do it because their institution encourages public engagement. Others do it because they want to make sure their research is accessible to as many readers as possible. Whatever your motivations, you need to have a clear idea of what they are before you get started. Your reasons might change as you go along, and that's fine.

But just a warning: if you go into this work seeking fame and fortune, you probably will be disappointed. There is hardly any money in public writing—at least not for the kind of writing that most people think of, that is, those short, interesting pieces you that appear online. And any fame you might gain from writing a piece that goes viral is fleeting at best, and dangerous at worst.

No. 3: Have I done the reading?

If you have written scholarly research, before you joined a new scholarly group or wrote for a new academic journal, you did some research about that group and you read that journal. That's just Being an Academic 101. And yet, over and over, newcomers to public writing submit pieces to publications they've rarely read, send in articles that don't meet the venue's submission guidelines, and draft essays that repeat (without attribution) arguments that have already been published.

In short, too many academic writers show no familiarity with the world into which they've entered.

If you want to write for the public, you have to become a part of the public you will be writing for. Read the magazines you want to write for. If you have a particular topic you want to write about, do some basic internet searching to see which journalists are experts on the topic, and then read everything those people have written about it lately. Just because others have already written on your topic doesn't mean you can't. It just means you have to cite them properly and say something new—or say something old in a new and compelling way.

The best part of reading is that you get more ideas for writing. You'll see what kind of conversations people are having, and you will find areas where you can contribute.

No. 4: What does my institution think?

Many smart academics have said many smart things about the institutional consequences of putting your ideas before the general public. In a recent essay, "Public Writing and the Junior Scholar," Sarah E. Bond and Kevin Gannon mount a convincing argument for public engagement as essential to the health of higher education: "We believe that the very survival of academe is, in part, predicated on encouraging both graduate students and junior scholars to engage in activities that speak to and for the public."[1] They argue that academe "must find effective ways to assess these pivotal forms of outreach" and offer some suggestions on that front.

While Bond and Gannon are optimistic about the positive influence that public writing can have on higher ed as a whole and on a young scholar's career in particular, other academics—particularly those from marginalized groups—have been more cautious, and with good reason. There is a risk of backlash. In fact, Bond herself faced a public backlash in 2017 for a piece she wrote about white supremacy.[2] All public writers risk backlash, whether they are in academia or not.

If you are still in higher ed, and the fallout turns ugly, you will need your institution's support. But can you count on it?

Public engagement has direr consequences for marginalized people, as sociologist and higher ed critic Tressie McMillan Cottom aptly points out.[3] If you are vulnerable faculty in higher education, such as a person of color or contingent faculty or both, think about how public engagement might put your job on the line. Cottom writes, "In this moment we should call for institutions to state explicitly what they owe those who venture into public waters." She notes: "Institutions have been calling for public scholarship for the obvious reasons. Attention can be equated with a type of prestige. And prestige is a way to shore up institutions when political and cultural attitudes are attacking colleges and universities at every turn." The trouble is, a lot of institutions aren't doing a good job of backing up their faculty when public engagement causes controversy which, as Cottom points out, is inevitable.

Will your institution support you if there is a backlash to something you write? To gauge that, do some research. Ask colleagues who have written for the public about their experiences. You can even ask the head of your division what their policy is.

At the very least, if you are still in higher ed, I recommend you get the answers two key questions. First, do you get professional credit for writing publicly? Second, will your institution stand by you if there are negative consequences to something you write?

If you are a freelance academic no longer in the academy, you won't get credit from an institution, and you won't have institutional support if you face backlash for something you've written. But at the same time, you won't have to worry about losing your job if something you said publicly annoys a Provost.

The best thing you can do as a freelance academic to shore up support in lieu of institutional support, is number 5, below.

No. 5: Have I found my writing peers?

If you are going to write for the public, you are going to need help from a community of peers who also write for the public. They will read your pitches and your pieces. They will refer you to editors.

They will spread the word about your latest work by sharing it on social media, direct messages, and email. They will also support you if (when) things go wrong, such as backlash to something you've written.

Every successful writer I know has a circle of peers providing support and encouragement. Public writing is a community-driven project. We need each other.

No. 6: Do I have to be on social media?

Yes, you need social media accounts. Twitter used to be *the* place for freelance writers. Since the Musk takeover, it's become less lively. Who knows what the future holds, but making sure readers can find your work is important, and social media is the springboard.

So swallow your objections and fears, join social media, and start engaging (politely!) in conversations. Listen to what others are saying about the topics you are interested in. Follow editors and see what they want to publish.

No. 7: Have I read the submission guidelines?

By this point, you've read the publication you want to write for. Next, turn your attention to the logistics: Do you know what the editors want in a pitch? Do they even publish freelance work? Do you know their guidelines for submitting something?

Writing for the public means learning a new trade called freelance writing. You can ask an experienced freelancer to teach you how to do it, but that is a really big ask, not only because they're really busy, but because the trade is complex. You can pay or barter with someone to teach you how to do it. This is more likely, as we are usually desperate for money. But your first step should be to research how to do it. (You've come to the right place.) You can often find panels on public writing at scholarly conferences, if you still attend those. Recently, the American Academy of Religion offered a panel on "Pitching to the Media."

The point is this. Don't start sending off pitches unless you're fairly certain you know what you're doing. There aren't that many publications out there, and editors talk to one another. If you come in looking like a rookie, that's potentially embarrassing but redeemable. If you come in behaving like an entitled jerk, no one will want to work with you. So read a publication's submission guidelines—more than once.

No. 8: Can I write a pitch?

A pitch is a highly specific genre. Sometimes people give entire workshops on how to write one because they're so complex. There is plenty of advice out there, including later in this book. I encourage you to do an internet search and find more.

No. 9: Am I prepared to share the credit?

When you write for general-interest publications, you usually don't have to worry about providing detailed footnotes, but that doesn't mean there are no citation norms. In public writing, citation is about two things: (1) giving nods to people whose work you leaned on to make your own argument and (2) building community.

When you're new, the world of freelance writing might seem vast. But once you've been in it for a while, it starts to shrink. And in this small world, everyone knows the names of those repeat offenders who fail to credit other writers when they should.

If you have something to say about an ongoing debate, dive in.

But remember that you're joining a public conversation already in progress. Show that you know who else is in it with you. Be respectful. Be kind. Be a good researcher.

And be mindful of who you are citing, and for what. Kecia Ali, a professor of religion at Boston University and a public writer, has researched the politics of citation and how it relates to gender, race, and ethnicity. Her findings, not surprisingly, show that marginalized people are cited less than white men.[4] Likewise, the Cite Black Women Collective pushes for equitable citation at the intersection of race and gender.[5]

As an eager rookie, you may have new and interesting things to say about a topic. But what you may fail to notice is that the new and interesting things you're saying have been touched on before, in similar ways, by other writers. Failing to point out these other ideas is one of the worst mistakes you can make as a new freelance writer. Remember this rule: If you can give a nod to someone who's written something on your topic already, do it. You'll look professional, you won't alienate anyone, and you'll build community in the process.

No. 10: Am I ready for this?

I learned one of the most important lessons about writing from Annie Dillard's book *The Writing Life*. It goes like this: If you have a good writing idea, use it now. Don't save it for later, for a better time, or for a better story or book or article. Or, as Dillard wrote: "One of the things I know about writing is this: Spend it all, shoot it, play it, lose it all, right away, every time."[6]

If you're ready to write for the public, don't wait till later. Don't wait for the perfect time. If you have the perfect words in mind, the perfect time to write them is now.

TWENTY-EIGHT

You Want to Write for the Public, but About What?

WHENEVER I'M APPROACHED BY CURRENT OR FORMER ACADEMICS who want to make the transition from scholarly to public writing, they always ask me the same question: "What should I write about?"

The answer to the question has two parts.

One part is about genre. Newcomers to public writing typically don't know the genres, that is, the differences between an op-ed, an essay, a profile, a reported article, or a well-researched think piece. You have to learn your journalism genres before you can decide which kind of piece to write (more about those genres in a future chapter).

The other part of the question has to do with figuring out what you have to contribute to public discourse. Once you've decided to broaden your reach beyond the scholarly realm, then comes the larger issue of what to say. How do you take your academic expertise and turn it into something that you, and your public, will want to read?

You can and should write about your research—but not just about it. In graduate school, we are trained to focus our scholarship narrowly. Eventually that limited focus helps us become experts and make new contributions to our subfield. The way academe defines expertise makes it hard to come by: If you haven't read *everything* on your topic, then you aren't an expert.

Therefore we end up being experts in very narrow things: We are not historians, or historians of U.S. history, or even historians of the Civil War, but rather, experts in military battles, aspects of slavery, or in Civil-War munitions. In my own scholarly writing, I wasn't an expert in English or law (my two doctoral degrees), but rather in rhetoric, and not just rhetoric but genre studies, and not just genre studies, but how genres can be a lens to view disability, and not just disability, but neurodiversity, until I ended up writing about such specialized topics as the genre of mental illness memoirs; the genre of mental-health reporting; the genre of mental-health reporting of mass shootings and how these things affect how gun laws are made. Wow. That's *really* narrow.

You must let go of this super-specialization mindset that scholars develop if you're going to write for the public. Your expertise as a public writer is broader than your scholarly expertise. In fact, one of the most freeing things about writing for the public is that you get to use your expertise in a larger context. You don't have to focus on Civil-War munitions anymore—you can write about the entire Civil War or move beyond even that topic and write about U.S. history more broadly.

So how do you make that transition? How do you go from a scholarly expert in something narrow to a public expert in something broader?

The answer is to stop thinking about your research and to start thinking about the world around you. Your inspiration for your public writing should come from what you are reading and seeing now, not from what you already know. Those of us who already write for nonacademic audiences were inspired to do so because we heard about some news story, public issue, or event and thought, "Because of my knowledge, I have something to say about that. I have something to contribute."

Public writing makes some academics nervous because they

don't trust that their expertise extends beyond their narrow scholarly niche. But it does out in the public sphere.

Here's an example from my own experience. After writing many scholarly articles about disability studies, I decided to branch into public writing about disability. I used my scholarly work as a foundation to leap from disability-studies scholar (narrow) to public writer on mental-health and disability (broad). Colleges debating whether to ban laptops from the classroom (again)? I wrote about that, because such bans create serious problems for students with disabilities. Another tragic shooting in which mental health gets used as a scapegoat to avoid banning guns? I wrote about that, too. (Even more tragically, more than once over the years.)

If you try to pitch a piece about your narrow slice of research to general-interest magazines or websites, it's highly unlikely to be published. There just won't be an audience for it, even if the publication covers higher education.

I interviewed Kelly J. Baker, former professor of religious studies and then-editor of *Women in Higher Education*.[1] She told me that she fields a lot of unsuccessful pitches from academics new to public writing. One of the most common mistakes they make, she said, is a failure to move beyond their scholarship: "Their pitch is too specific to their discipline. They rely on too much jargon or write a pitch that would be a better fit for an academic journal rather than a magazine."

To succeed in public writing, then, you have to take that brave first step beyond the small but safe territory of your scholarly expertise. Use your academic training as a foundation and then do the additional research and reporting necessary to write a journalistic piece. Use current events as the driving force of your freelance writing, and your expertise follows.

Mind Your Audience

Once you start writing for the public, keep reminding yourself that your audience has changed, drastically. That shift in audience means you have to shift your language, your persona, your tone, or however you wish to describe the writing choices you make for different types of readers. It involves more than just dropping the academic jargon.

Kevin Kruse, a professor of history, has written trade books for popular audiences and many, many op-eds and essays for public venues. In an interview, I asked him about how to successfully switch from writing for a scholarly to a popular audience. His first piece of advice is to keep in mind who your audience is: "A successful op-ed is one aimed at an 'intelligent audience of nonspecialists,'" he said, noting he's heard that same phrase from many different editors for years.[2]

How does he approach writing for a public audience? "I've found that constructing a piece much as I would a lecture for my undergraduate survey is the best route to take," he said. In that vein, Kruse follows three general practices. First, "Write with clarity," using plain language and avoiding academic jargon. Second, include "clear examples." Finally, assume your audience is interested in your topic but doesn't know much about it.

Make It Relevant

Your starting point in deciding what to write is not your research, but current events. No editor will care about your vast knowledge unless you can make that knowledge relevant to what is happening right now. When you pitch pieces that editors will actually want to publish, you must tie your expertise to the present moment.

Sarah Bond, a professor of history and a public writer, gives this advice in an essay she wrote for academics-turned-public writers: "React to the world we are living in."[3] Why? Because, she writes, that's how you figure out what to write about: "Did you see a parallel with Cicero in Trump's State of the Union rhetoric last night? Write about it. Are there early Christian saints who had similar #metoo moments to women of today? Write about it."

You need a "news peg"—journalism-speak for an angle that makes your article timely. Alternatively, your topic might be "evergreen"—journalism-speak for a topic that is always of public interest, in which case you must point that out in your pitch.

As Baker told me, "Timeliness and relevancy matter" in a pitch. Pay attention to current events, she said: "When what you study appears in the news cycle, be ready to pitch an idea quickly. Look at what publications publish and how your area of expertise might fit into their coverage."

Kruse has similar advice: "A successful pitch is one that has an obvious 'hook'—a connection to the news cycle then unfolding—and virtually no newspaper or magazine will want to run a piece that lacks that hook." And don't bury your hook in your pitch letter, he said. "The hook needs to be laid out quite simply and directly in the opening paragraph." Never make an editor guess why your piece is relevant; it should be apparent in the very first sentence.

If all of this sounds like fast-paced work compared with scholarly articles, it is. Be prepared to pitch and write quickly. For a fast-unfolding news peg, a turnaround time of 24 hours isn't unusual.

Stepping into the public arena can be intimidating and even scary, but the skills you need to be successful in it can be learned. From now on, when you read your favorite websites or magazines, read them as a potential writer, not just as a consumer. Start thinking about ways you can contribute to the publication. And perhaps, someday soon, your name will be in the byline.

TWENTY-NINE

The Venue, the Pitch, and the Fee

SO YOU'VE DECIDED IT'S TIME TO TAKE YOUR SCHOLARSHIP OUT FROM behind the paywalls and write for the public. After mulling how your expertise relates to something in the news, you have a sense of what to write. You even have some venues in mind. Now what?

How, exactly, do you approach editors at newspapers, magazines, and websites? What do you say? And what are the next steps if an editor accepts your pitch?

You might have a vague sense of how the process usually works: You pitch an idea to editors, who either accept or reject it and sometimes ignore it entirely. Some editors give you feedback once they accept the pitch: include a little more of this or a little more of that; check out this story or interview that source. Then you and the editor come to an agreement about length, deadline, and fee.

Spoiler alert: Most of the time, you'll get very little say about any of those things.

All of that editorial back-and-forth can be nerve-wracking, especially if you're new to public writing, and even when you're not. In this chapter, I will spell out the things you have to do before you get serious about the actual writing.

Finding Editors

When you're used to approaching a specific set of scholarly journals, it can be a strange experience figuring out how to find—let alone communicate with—editors of public venues. Scholarly journals seem to move at a snail's pace, while websites, magazines, and newspapers are fast-paced environments where editors are under a lot of time pressure.

For a freelance writer, creating and maintaining relationships with editors is crucial to your success. Cold-emailing can work when you pitch a story to an editor, but you'll have more success if you use your professional network. Either you get a referral from another writer or editor, or best of all, you pitch an editor for whom you've written before.

For insights on how to connect with editors, I interviewed Liz Bucar, a professor of philosophy and religion and project lead of Sacred Writes: Public Scholarship on Religion.[1] How, I asked, had she gotten her foot in the door when she started public writing? She pointed out that she had help—which is not uncommon: "I was extremely lucky with my last publisher, Harvard University Press, whose ace marketing team reached out to editors on my behalf."

However, Bucar said, making the introduction to a magazine or website editor was all that the marketing team did. She had to establish and maintain the professional relationships on her own: "Once they had an editor interested, it was up to me to pitch, write, and respond to editorial feedback quickly—which I did."

Early on, Bucar said, she also teamed up with a freelance journalist on a project: "One of the best things I've done to learn about public writing is co-report a series on Muslim feminist activism with Amanda Randone, a freelance journalist." Bucar learned a lot through that partnership: "We did everything together—developed pitches, conducted interviews, wrote, and edited." She credits the collaboration with giving her much of her insider knowledge about freelancing: "That experience taught me a lot about the culture of journalism, the craft of writing for a public audience, but also the norms of interacting with busy high-powered editors."

Learning those norms is crucial to success in freelance writing. Bucar now shares what she knows via Sacred Writes, which offers an annual training retreat for academics to learn the ins and outs of public writing directly from reporters and editors. "Never underestimate what you can learn—just by being in the room—about the pressure a media outlet is under, the way they frame stories, and how their audience is evolving," Bucar said.

But what if you don't have access to a retreat, or to a publisher that can help you make connections with editors? How do you get started on your own?

That was my predicament back in 2014, when I was just starting to write for public venues. The few connections I had to mainstream publications came not from academe but from social media—mainly Twitter. It was scary the first time I asked someone I "knew" only from Twitter to refer me to her editor, but she did it (and gladly), and my public-writing career was born.

Bucar agrees that social media is essential for scholars who want to write for the public: "A lot of relationship-building between scholars and editors happens on Twitter. I know scholars not on Twitter hate to hear this, but it is true: If you want to be networking with editors, the best way is to be active on Twitter." Since my interview with Bucar, Twitter has been taken over by Elon Musk and has drastically changed. You can still find editors there, but the network of writers has grown less lively. I encourage you to also create a profile on Linked In, where many writers have begun discussing their work. I also encourage you to research how to cultivate the best online presence for a freelance writer.

Pitching Your Idea

Once you've established which editors you will approach, and how, you have to sell your story to them. You sell your story with a "pitch." In her advice essay, "How to Craft a Pitch," Kelly J. Baker, former professor of religious studies and then-editor of *Women in Higher Education*, writes, "Pitching a potential article to any publication involves a delicate balance. You must tell the editor what the article is about, show how the article would fit the publication, and explain why you are qualified to write said article before writing the whole darn thing."[2] The hardest part, Baker adds, is brevity: "You must accomplish all of that in a few paragraphs, which can seem daunting." A good pitch is just long enough to "offer a glimpse of your voice as a writer as well as the tone of the article, so the editor can decide how you fit (or don't) with the publication's style, tone, and approach."

Remember, a good pitch makes an impression on editors even if they reject it. An editor is more likely to remember you the next time you send them an idea, or even take the initiative and contact you. Creating a good relationship with an editor can be done even with a rejected pitch, and a good relationship means that pitching becomes easier in the future.

Don't be surprised if the initial reaction you get from an editor is skepticism. Fair or not, Bucar told me, "Scholars have a reputation of being entitled and difficult. That is how a lot of editors think of us." That's a hill you may have to climb in order to build trust. So, she added, "prove them wrong. Be polite, respectful, helpful, and, above all else, kind. This matters." A simple thank you is always a good idea.

And don't get discouraged by rejection; it's just part of the process. Keep a positive attitude and use the rejection as an opportunity to show that you are a professional. Be gracious to the editor who rejected your idea (after all, many editors don't reply at all). After the rejection, rework the pitch and send it to another venue—and then another and another, until you've placed it. If it's good, it will find a home.

As you form more relationships with editors, this process will get easier. Many times a pitch from an unknown writer is rejected because they don't know how good a writer you are. Once you've gained an editor's trust, you may not need to pitch at all. Instead, they'll come to you with an idea for you to write. That's when you know you've made it.

Talking About Fees

Once an editor accepts your pitch, you naturally want to know about the money. I know I did when I started freelancing, mostly because I was moving out of higher education and into the position of a freelance academic at the time, and I constantly worried about money.

The first thing to know is that you probably will not earn much from your freelance writing. I learned early on that I could not make a living solely from writing for the public. But I could use it to supplement my income.

What kind of money can you expect for a freelance piece in a mainstream publication? "For an op-ed of 700 to 800 words, I have made everything from $125 to $350," said Bucar.

In my experience, those rates are pretty standard. If you want to learn more about how much you can expect to be paid, ask your own freelance writer colleagues. You also can check the crowdsourced website Who Pays Writers? (whopayswriters.com) for more information on what different publications pay for freelance pieces. And once you start publishing, submit your rates to that site. Its database is only as strong as the information we provide.

If you are a full-time academic with a steady income, you may decide to write without pay for smaller publications in order to get "clips," journalism-speak for published pieces. But think twice before agreeing to write for free. As Bucar told me, "Even if I don't need to be paid, it is important to others that I not provide unpaid labor in cases where publications can afford to pay me."

If a fee is low—be sure you understand what "low" means—you can request a higher one. Freelance writers do negotiate. Especially if you've been writing for a publication for a while, it is normal to request a higher fee, just as you'd ask your employer for a raise.

But what if the publication is nonprofit? In that case, allowing it to publish your work without paying you might make sense. Often, these small publications are run by and for marginalized groups and have trouble securing funding. The editors often work for free in order to get the writing of marginalized writers to the public. These publications wish they could pay their writers, but marginalized writers and their publications do not have the same funding as CNN dot com.

I can't say this enough: Don't be afraid to talk about money. If a colleague asks you how much you made writing that essay for CNN or *Vox*, please share that information. Help your colleague negotiate a higher rate. Remember, that person might be in a position to return the favor in the future.

THIRTY

Public Writing in Uncertain Times

WHEN TIMES ARE UNCERTAIN OR IN UPHEAVAL, IT CAN BE HARD TO write for the public. A contentious presidential election (or presidency), tragic natural disasters, wars, pandemics. These events govern much of what we do as well as what we read. If you work in or adjacent to higher education and read about higher-ed topics, then you are mostly reading about how institutions are handling these topics.

Under difficult conditions, it can be harder than ever to write for the public. If you are under stress yourself, it can be a struggle to formulate a pitch or to find the motivation to write at all. Maybe you want to write about a topic that is important to you, but the news outlets are fixated on singular topics that are dominating the news cycle even though it would be better for public discourse if they would broaden their coverage.

In other words, writing in uncertain times can be both hard on your mental health and frustrating for your career.

Why Are You Writing for the Public Now?

During uncertain times, I cope by writing. I write in private journal entries, social media threads, or essays for my own blog.

In other words, I write in places where I don't have to interact with editors, but I can still interact with the public. During the height of the Covid pandemic, I wrote essays about how living in a pandemic has affected me and my anxiety disorder and about homeschooling and taking it easy on yourself as a parent, since I'm a homeschooler by choice and had advice to give.

I didn't write those pieces because I felt a need to be "productive"—quite the opposite, and I didn't write them to get paid. After all, they were published on my blog, which doesn't generate money. No, I wrote them because I couldn't stop thinking about how much my life has changed along with everyone else's. I quite literally couldn't get the thoughts from my mind. Writing helped me gain perspective on events so large they seemed to defy perspective. I didn't submit them to public venues because of sheer exhaustion. After I'd finished writing the essays, the thought of pitching, submitting to editors, and revising seemed too much.

As a public writer, experienced or not, you have lots of options for publishing your work. "Publish" simply means "to make public." Establishing a blog and publishing your work in that venue creates a space that can feel safe when you are writing about subjects that are personal or exploratory. Publishing on a blog is also a way to get something out there when you don't have the mental energy to go through the pitching and editing processes.

Moving the Personal to the Public

Sometimes the personal story you have to tell might change the world for the better, and you want to publish it in a traditional venue so that you will reach a larger audience. The genre you will write is called a "personal essay."

In an interview, Erin Celello, a novelist and creative writing professor, shared with me the story of co-writing an essay with her husband Aaron Olver during the Covid pandemic.[1] The essay told the story of her husband's serious illness during the H1N1 influenza pandemic a decade before. The illness put him in a coma and on a ventilator. After publishing the essay in a public venue, the article went viral.

Why write publicly about her husband's illness at all? Celello told me that she wanted to advocate for the seriousness of COVID-19 and the importance of social distancing. She said, "Somehow, we've found ourselves in the midst of a global pandemic that has been weirdly politicized." Where she lives, in Wisconsin, people "think this is a problem for urban areas, and that the solutions to it are being unduly levied on them." She described how "thousands of people jammed themselves onto the lawn of the capitol to protest safer-at-home restrictions." In writing their essay, she and her husband hoped they "might encourage people to think a bit about why we're doing this [staying at home], even though it's decimating our economy and so many people's livelihoods."

But publishing the piece wasn't easy for Celello. Their story spread rapidly across social media and garnered a lot of attention. "We're both pretty private people," she said, "and I wasn't prepared for all of the emotions that sharing our story brought up." Ultimately, she was glad they published the essay: "We both felt it was important in light of all the misinformation and apparent controversy surrounding protection measures that local and state governments have taken."

Plus, as a novelist, Celello understood the power of storytelling when it comes to persuading people to change their behavior: "We hoped a personal angle might be effective in helping people see what was at risk, even if those risks seemed far away or deceptively small—mathematically speaking." In other words, by telling a personal story, Celello brought the risks of Covid-19 up close to her readers in a bid to convince them to keep themselves and their community safe.

Finding a Personal Angle on a Big Subject

It can be intimidating to find something new to say on a big topic when so much has been said already. As Celello's story shows, using a personal essay to make a point about something larger is one way to do so.

Another conundrum you might face is that you want to write about something that isn't a Very Big Thing lately but is still important. Or perhaps it is an angle on the Very Big Thing but has been ignored by media outlets in favor of flashier topics.

A hard lesson you must learn about writing for general-interest publications is that if the topic isn't timely, then no editor will publish your article. That's just how public writing works. If you don't have a news peg—an angle that makes your topic newsworthy—then no editor will touch your story. Why would they? They are looking for timely, relevant, compelling, potentially influential pieces that lots of people will want to read. That's how they make money.

But don't despair. Within the topic of a Very Big Thing lies an infinite number of angles—including ones that you want to write about. You just need to convince an editor that they should publish it because it is, you guessed it, timely, relevant, compelling, and potentially influential.

So how do you convince editors to publish your piece even though it may be an unorthodox approach to the Very Big Thing?

First, do your research. There's no point pitching a piece to a publication if your exact angle has already been the subject of a recent piece. Consider how to join a conversation that's already in progress. When writing about a Very Big Thing, finding out what's already been said is more important than ever. Also, even in your pitch, be sure to cite others who have already started conversations you are joining because public writing is a community.

Second, pitch even if the outlet ran something similar on your topic. Your odds of getting published improve if you can find a way to build on what's been published on the topic before. Help the editor see that what you have to say furthers a debate already in progress because that makes your piece even more timely.

Third, write a strong pitch and be persistent. Keep a positive attitude, and don't get snippy if you're rejected—after all, you might want to pitch that venue again. If you use the rejection as an opportunity to show you are a professional, you're more likely to get a positive response next time. Don't be discouraged by rejection; it's just part of the process. Revise your pitch and send it to the next venue on your list. (You should have a list.)

If you feel safe pitching stories on Very Big Things which, as Celello's story shows, is a concern you should consider, then step into the fray. As freelance academics, we have the training to take on complex subjects and make them understandable to public audiences in a thoughtful fashion. That vital skill is in short supply at times when we need it most.

THIRTY-ONE

How to Lose an Editor in Five Days

IF YOU'RE NEW TO WRITING FOR THE PUBLIC, YOU CAN FEEL LIKE you're entering a world where everyone knows a secret handshake but you.

You are correct (if not literally).

There are, indeed, expected ways of communicating with editors of public venues that you can't possibly know unless someone tells you—or you learn the hard way by making mistakes. You would probably prefer to avoid making those mistakes.

In previous chapters, I've taught you how to avoid as many mistakes as you can when you first start interacting with editors. I've helped you learn how to build relationships with editors because relationships make writing for the public so much easier. If you build relationships with editors, when you have new stories to pitch, your pitches are more likely to be accepted. Editors enjoy working with writers with whom they are familiar. If they know your writing style, your work ethic, and how easy you are to work with, they're more likely to accept your pitch. If they know you turn in clean copy, take criticism well, and file on time, then your pitch will get closer consideration.

But this chapter isn't going to teach you any of these things.

Instead, it will teach you how to burn relationships with editors from the get-go. I interviewed two excellent editors and drew from my own experience in order to give you the worst advice possible.

So, look no further, dear reader. Here is all you need to know about how to lose an editor in five days.

Day 1. Don't Research the Editor or the Venue

Editors strongly prefer it when you pitch a story that is a good fit for their magazine. Therefore, if you want to lose your editor, don't research the venue, and for good measure, don't research the editor, either.

I interviewed Evette Dionne, the now-former Editor-in-Chief of Bitch Media, about her favorite things writers do. She told me, "I can always tell when a writer has actually read our publication, knows our tone, and knows the kind of content we publish."[1] As Dionne explained, the best pitches really fit a publication.

If you want to lose an editor, make sure your topic, tone, length, or genre don't fit the venue you are pitching.

Editors also dislike being called "editor" in your pitch when their names are right there on the masthead. It's not the worst thing in the world that you can do, but failing to use the editor's name shows that you haven't done strong research about the venue.

Another reason to research the editors is to figure out which editor handles the pitches of the type you are submitting. Larger publications have editors for different topics or types of pieces. To be successful, you need to be sure you are sending your pitch to the right person.

In short: The best writers do their research about a venue and its editors before they ever sit down to pitch.

So, if you want to lose your editor—ignore the publication completely. Don't even read it. And definitely don't find out who the editors are. You'll lose your editor on day one. Excellent work!

Day 2. Ignore the Submission Guidelines

Oh no! It's day two, and you haven't lost your editor yet. Don't worry, there's still time. All you have to do is ignore the submission guidelines.

Submission guidelines are the instructions that editors carefully put together to instruct prospective authors about how to pitch to and write for their magazines. Guidelines are crucial to the operation of a magazine. When wading through a vast number of submissions, the guidelines help editors figure out, quickly, what kind of piece is being pitched, whether it is timely (that means "urgent"), which editor to pass it on to, and more.

Editors put a lot of thought into their submission guidelines. In an interview, Kelly J. Baker, former professor of religious studies and then-editor of *Women in Higher Education,* described to me the effort she spent writing her magazine's guidelines: "As editor, I took the time to describe the audience of my publication, the style and voice, the word count...and the types of articles that I actually publish. I even have a guideline on how to write a proper pitch."[2] After all of that effort, when a writer ignores an editor's guidelines, an editor can tell that a writer is unprofessional. In fact, many editors won't even read a pitch if it strays too far from the guidelines. Editors can tell the difference between a writer who made an honest mistake and one who didn't bother to look.

On the other hand, someone who takes the time to study and follow the guidelines can win an editor's respect. In fact, Baker told me that carefully reading her guidelines is one way to win her editorial heart: "When a writer, freelance or academic, emails me a pitch for an article, and I can tell they not only looked at the submission guidelines but read some articles, I sort of swoon. It's a beautiful thing."

If you want to lose your editor, dear reader, don't make them swoon. Ignore submission guidelines, and you will lose your editor by day two, guaranteed.

Day 3. Write a Terrible Pitch

Yikes! It's day three, and you still haven't lost your editor. What do you do now? Don't worry, you still have to write your pitch, and you can write a really bad one.

Dionne told me that she "really appreciate[s] writers who send over fleshed-out pitches that explain what their idea is, why it's the best fit for *Bitch*, and why they are the best person to write it." So, if you're going to write a good pitch, you have three things you need to cover:

(1) Your piece's **idea.**

(2) your piece's "**fit**" with the venue.

(3) your piece's **writer** (you!).

Sometimes Dionne receives a good idea lodged in a bad pitch, and she has to turn the pitch down: "It is not ideal to receive the germ of an idea of a writer because I don't always have time to help writers flesh out their thoughts. I feel bad declining pitches that are simply not as thorough as they could or should be, but that's the reality." Thus, a good pitch goes into enough detail so that the editor has a clear picture of what the finished piece will be.

The advice I give to new writers is to start with three main points about your topic: your argument, your angle, and your assessment of the current conversation. If you touch on those three things, you'll have substance to your pitch.

Also, editors prefer it when writers are polite in their emails. Baker told me, "Being kind and courteous in a first email is a must. Show your enthusiasm and that you can be a team player." So in addition to the three things you need to cover in a pitch, you need to be respectful, kind, and polite.

From my experience as a freelance writer, I can tell you that addressing a magazine editor by their first name is just fine, but you should still use a formal salutation such as "Dear." If you were pitching to me, then, "Dear Katie" would be a fine way to address me in an email. However, I don't enjoy receiving pitches addressed in this way: "Dear Mark." My name is not Mark.

When editors receive pitches addressed incorrectly, they know that they've received a cut-and-pasted pitch. A cut-and-pasted pitch alerts an editor that the writer has likely not researched the publication. An incorrectly addressed pitch also indicates that the writer doesn't pay attention to detail, which is never a good thing.

A cut-and-pasted pitch might raise an editor's ire, but things can get worse, as Baker explains: "I receive emails from folks who have a good idea for an article but are complete jerks to me. They're arrogant, condescending, or mean."

So, dear reader, how do you lose an editor when you're pitching? Simple! (1) Make sure your piece's main idea is incomprehensible or vague. (2) Fail to explain why the piece fits the venue. (3) Don't explain why you are a good person to write it. (4) And finally, be sloppy and rude.

Just follow these instructions, and you will be sure to lose your editor on day three.

Day 4. Don't Accept Revisions

I don't know what to tell you.

It's day four, and you still haven't lost your editor. That means you have researched your venue and editor, you've carefully read and followed the submission guidelines, and you've written a strong pitch that is not only polite but also strongly outlines your piece's idea, your piece's fit, and why you're the best writer for your piece. How do you expect to lose your editor if you do everything well?

You can still lose your editor, but you have your work cut out for you. It's time to ramp up your efforts. You must be a jerk when your editor asks for revisions.

Dionne shared that she "enjoy[s] writers who turn in clean copy on time." As a new public writer, especially one transitioning from higher ed where deadlines are much slower and looser, understand that public venues are operating under deadlines far tighter than the ones that you have been accustomed to in the past. Instead of months'-long turnaround times, online venues have turnaround times measured in hours.

Thus, new public writers should take both parts of Dionne's advice seriously if they want to be successful: (1) When you turn in your writing, it needs to be as print-ready as you can possibly make it. Your editor needs to focus on content, not grammar or style. (2) You need to meet your deadlines, and even beat them if you can. No editor ever complained about a piece being filed early. They might not be able to edit it early, but it's a relief to know that a piece is already turned in and that they don't have to run it down.

Once you've filed your piece, you will most likely receive edits. If you're new to public writing, you will *definitely* receive edits. As Dionne says, "Collaboration is crucial to producing a thorough piece, so writers have to be open to that." Dionne points out that it is difficult to work with a writer who doesn't understand the editorial process: "Edits are not suggestions, but they can be tweaked based on the writer's preferences. Rejecting every single edit is just not ideal, especially when working with an editor for the first time."

Baker shares similar opinions: "A writer doesn't have to accept all edits on an article, and I'm open to talking about things that writers want to keep. I'm not open to writers who want to fight about every single edit and assume that they know more about my job than I do."

(Readers: You do not know more about an editor's job than they do.)

Here is a losing-your-editor no-brainer: File your piece late and full of errors, and then reject or fight about every suggestion your editor makes.

Follow my advice, and you will lose your editor faster than the Road Runner loses Wile E. Coyote.

Day 5. Be Rude When Your Pitch Is Rejected

If you've made it all the way to day five and you haven't lost your editor, don't lose hope. This is your Hail-Mary opportunity to alienate an editor forever.

Suppose your pitch is rejected. What should you do? Should you reply politely, thanking the editor for their time and use the opportunity to build a strong relationship? Or should you dash off and angry email and burn that relationship forever so that you can never pitch that venue or editor again?

Baker has dealt with many reactions to rejection. She tells me, "Writers respond to rejection in a lot of different ways. [As a writer,] I hate having an article rejected because it feels personal to me. It's not personal though, so don't act like it is." It can be really hard to separate our personal selves from our writing, but if we are going to be professional writers, then we have to do so. If your pitch or story is rejected, the rejection is not a reflection on you as a person. Most often, it has nothing to do with you at all.

Baker has good advice for how to respond to rejection: "The most effective way to respond is a quick 'Thank you for considering this article' email, even when you don't want to send it." It can be hard to send that gracious email when you're stinging with rejection, but you need to do it anyway. Your graciousness can pay off. Baker explains: "Remember what a writer is trying to do is build a relationship with an editor." So the best writers suck it up and send that thank you email.

The ones who don't? Baker has plenty of experience in that department: "Sending me an email telling me that I'm stupid for rejecting your article isn't the way to go. ... Asking me to explain my decision is also not the best approach. I don't have to accept the pitch you send me, and I don't have to explain why I decided to pass on it. Sending me an ALL CAPS email to contest my rejection is the fastest way to guarantee that I won't work with you now or in the future."

There you have it, readers! The best advice, straight from the editor's mouth. Hit that caps-lock key and express your anger at being rejected, and you'll lose your editor forever.

Alternatively, you can do the opposite of everything above. You can take the advice Dionne and Baker have given you and use it to share your writing via public venues. You can form excellent relationships with editors and write like seasoned professionals.

Epilogue: Finding Stability as a Freelance Academic

WHEN I STARTED WRITING ABOUT BEING A FREELANCE ACADEMIC, I was a Ph.D. on leave from my contingent faculty job—trying to figure out how to find a fulfilling career in a higher-education system that did not value my work. The solution, I ultimately decided, was to value myself, leave higher education, and create work that I liked.

Skip forward from 2014 to now, and I've left academe, started my freelancing business, and created a relatively stable life for myself doing work that I (usually) enjoy. But the key word in that sentence is "stable." Too many faculty-turned-freelancers have trouble finding stability, especially now that more and more work across all fields is outsourced from full-time positions to what has been dubbed the "gig economy." Those of us living from job to job know that freelancing can give your nerves a drubbing. I, for one, didn't leave the stress of a contingent job to live an even more unstable life. Here's how I found stability as a freelance academic.

Put Safeties in Place

For me, at least, the news cycle has been exhausting ever since 2016 because of the presidential administration, COVID-19, election crises, and horrible wars. Every day, it seems, there's a new terrible thing. Just living through it has been hard. I know that others feel the same.

As a freelance journalist, though, the news cycle has been a particular kind of wrecking ball. I'm someone who is paid to write about those horrifying things, and I'm beginning to hate that slice of my freelance work. It's hard to write in-depth coverage of an event when, 24 hours later, my work might well be out of date. And when I try to write a story that keeps up with the news cycle, it's even more exhausting than usual. Everything else I'm working on (not to mention my private life) must be put on hold to write it. Before the current administration (at the time of this writing, Trump was in office) and its incessant horror, a quick turnaround on a reported piece might be three or four days. Now? The turnaround time is twenty-four hours at most, and, even then, the magazine might kill your story because something more atrocious has happened in the meantime.

And that's just my freelance journalism work. There's also the rest of my career that I cobble together through freelance consulting, editing, and more. I never know how much money will come in each month, and when I'll strike it big—relatively speaking. Basically, working as a freelancer can be exhausting because it can feel like you're always on a financial roller-coaster. The freedom and flexibility are huge pluses, but the sheer unpredictability of it can wear you out.

I've learned how to put safeties in place to create a more stable life as a freelancer. Stability is not just about bringing in a consistent income. It's also about generating consistent work and creating a community I can count on. Those three things—consistent money, work, and community—are the three legs of the table I'm building my freelance career on now. Whether you are an academic thinking about starting a side business, or you are leaving higher education entirely, here are some things to consider about each of those legs.

Stable, Consistent Money

It is a truism of freelancing that getting paid is hard. Our clients often sit on our money. Just because you've done the work doesn't mean that you'll have your money. So it is your job to ensure that you have money and aren't, therefore, at the mercy of clients who can't or won't pay you on time.

Here's a trick I learned from a friend, mentor, and writer, Claire McGuire. It was some of the best freelancing advice I've ever received: Pay yourself a paycheck each month. Keep the amount consistent and keep it within the means of your business.

This trick requires having two checking accounts. One is your business account. This is the account where the income from your clients goes—and from which you draw your regular paycheck. The other account is your personal account, and that's where you deposit your paycheck. Send yourself a paycheck each month, and make sure the amount is the same every month and always well within your means.

If you follow these rules, you will have a predictable income because you will always know how much you will "make" each month. Even though the amount in your business account might fluctuate, your paycheck stays the same. One month your business might make a lot. But the next month it might make less. That's okay because your paycheck is stable. Earlier in this book, I describe how to set up business checking accounts and other business details. Be sure to read those chapters before you start your business.

When I was first getting started as a freelancer, my monthly paycheck amount was low. That's because what I had in the bank was low, and I didn't know what to expect in the future. I had no financial cushion. Now that I've been doing this for a while, the monthly paycheck amount has grown—slightly. I can look at what I have in the bank and project forward as I give myself a steady paycheck.

Honestly, a steady paycheck, no matter how small, is

something that every freelancer dreams of—or at least this freelancer does. As you find stability as a freelance academic, get off the income roller-coaster as quickly as you can.

Stable, Consistent Work

Finding consistent work is the hobgoblin of all freelancers. The examples I provide are for a freelance writer, but the concepts will work for you in whatever self-employment you are pursuing.

When I first started freelance writing, I got some good advice from a writer friend: once you've pitched an idea and written for a magazine, she said, you pitch a series next. In other words, take the one stand-alone piece of work and turn it into predictable, consistent work.

In general terms, take a one-off paycheck and transform it into a steady income stream.

At the beginning of my freelance career, I did that twice. I wrote a single piece, then on the basis of that single piece, pitched the editor a column. Both times, the editor said yes. With those yeses, I had my first steady, predictable work. The lesson I learned there was this: whenever I write for a magazine, and the editors seem to like what I've produced, I pitch a continuing column on the subject. Often, they say no, but sometimes they say yes. Sometimes they just buy the sample pitches I suggest, or they keep me on tap as a go-to person for a certain beat. But those things are good outcomes, too.

To look at this in a bigger-picture fashion, the idea here is to standardize the services you offer—whether they are editing services, technical skills you learned in graduate school, or some independent skill you pursued on your own. What I mean is this: don't just do piecemeal work for piecemeal clients. You don't want to be cold-pitching all the time, because that requires doing two tasks: building trust with a new client as well as selling your services. Finding a way to turn the first job you do for a client into a continuing source of paid work cuts out the first task (building trust) and lets you skip straight to the second.

Two final notes about building consistent work.

First, if you do successful work for clients, ask them for two things in return: a testimonial (have them email it to you so you have it in writing) and referrals. Put the testimonial on your website and on whatever social media you use, such as a Google Business or Facebook Business page.

Second, always have a clean, up-to-date résumé ready as a safety net. Sometimes you need to bow out of freelancing for a while, and there's nothing wrong with that.

Stable, Consistent Community

I knew, of course, that freelance work meant going it alone, but I was nonetheless surprised by just how lonely this sort of work can be. I spend so much of my time alone—even more than was the case in graduate school or when I was teaching. I'm fortunate, however. I stumbled, very much by accident, into a virtual and long-distance community of like-minded freelancers.

While I found my community of freelancer colleagues by accident, maintaining those relationships is something I do very deliberately. I try to schedule videochats and phone calls after I meet people via social media and work hard not to let the connections lapse. I keep a calendar and ensure that I stay in touch with my fellow freelancers regularly. Indeed, I call them "colleagues," because that is what they are. Although I don't go to work at an office or a department, they are colleagues with whom I share my career failures and successes and upon whom I depend for support. I look out for them, and they look out for me. The stability of that community is the heart of my freelancing career.

I've managed to create a career I can (mostly) count on, which, in the grand scheme of things, is all I could wish for.

I wish the same for you.

Notes

Introduction to the Revised and Expanded Edition

1. Rebecca Pope-Ruark, *Unraveling Faculty Burnout: Pathways to Reckoning and Renewal* (Baltimore: Johns Hopkins University Press, 2022), https://doi.org/10.56021/9781421445137, 6.
2. Lisa M. Jaremka et al., "Common Academic Experiences No One Talks About: Repeated Rejection, Impostor Syndrome, and Burnout," *Perspectives on Psychological Science* 15, no. 3 (May 1, 2020): 520, https://doi.org/10.1177/1745691619898848.
3. Katie Rose Guest Pryal, "Disclosure Blues: Should You Tell Colleagues About Your Mental Illness," *The Chronicle of Higher Education*, June 13, 2014, http://dx.doi.org/10.2139/ssrn.4158926, also included in Pryal, *Life of the Mind Interrupted*.
4. Joseph Fruscione and Kelly J. Baker, "Introduction," in *Succeeding Outside the Academy: Career Paths beyond the Humanities, Social Sciences, and STEM*, ed. Joseph Fruscione and Kelly J. Baker (Lawrence: University Press of Kansas, 2018), 1–7; American Federation of Teachers, "An Army of Temps: AFT Contingent Faculty Quality of Work/Life Report 2022," 2022, https://www.aft.org/sites/default/files/media/documents/2023/Contingent_Faculty_Survey_2022_interactive.pdf.
5. Gretchen M. Reevy and Grace Deason, "Predictors of Depression, Stress, and Anxiety among Non-Tenure Track Faculty," *Frontiers in Psychology* 5, no. 701 (July 8, 2014): 1–17, https://doi.org/10.3389/fpsyg.2014.00701.
6. Katie Rose Guest Pryal, "Front-Line Faculty and Systemic Burnout: Why More Faculty Should Attend to Law Students' Mental Health and the Inequities Caused by Faculty Who Opt Out," *Legal Writing: The Journal of the Legal Writing Institute* 27, no. 1 (2023): 201.
7. Academic Misconduct Database, "Incidents," accessed August 15, 2024, https://perma.cc/HCJ9-JZJW.
8. Bret Devereaux, "Academic Ranks Explained Or What On Earth Is an Adjunct?," *A Collection of Unmitigated Pedantry*, April 28, 2023, https://acoup.blog/2023/04/28/collections-academic-ranks-explained-or-what-on-earth-is-an-adjunct/.

1. A Manifesto for the Freelance Academic

1. Kelly J. Baker, "To Write Or Not To Write," *Chronicle Vitae*, September 9, 2014, https://perma.cc/CG5D-ZZAE.
2. Rebecca Shuman, *The Chronicle of Higher Education*, "Hanging Up on a Calling," (Jan. 27, 2014), Jacqui Shine, *Chronicle Vitae*, "Love and Other

Notes

Secondhand Emotions" (Feb. 3, 2014), William Pannapacker, *The Chronicle of Higher Education*, "On Graduate School and 'Love'" (Oct. 1, 2013).
3. Sarah Kendzior, "Should Academics Write for Free?" *Chronicle Vitae*, October 14, 2013, https://perma.cc/5G9T-CGG9.
4. Elizabeth Keenan, "The No-Baby Penalty," *Chronicle Vitae*, June 19, 2014, https://perma.cc/W569-Z935.
5. Rebecca Schuman, "Thesis Hatement," *Slate*, April 5, 2013, https://perma.cc/YPP6-WRY4.

2. What Does It Mean to Be a Freelance Academic?

1. Rebecca Schuman, "My Academic Metamorphosis," The Chronicle of Higher Education, May 13, 2013, https://www.chronicle.com/article/my-academic-metamorphosis/.
2. Thomas Hammond et al., "The Prevalence of Failure-Based Depression Among Elite Athletes," *Clinical Journal of Sport Medicine* 23, no. 4 (July 2013): 273–77, https://doi.org/10.1097/JSM.0b013e318287b870.

3. On Not Writing

1. Monterey County Herald, "NJ College: Professor Fired for Making Racially Insensitive Remarks," *Monterey County Herald*, June 24, 2017, https://www.montereyherald.com/2017/06/24/nj-college-professor-fired-for-racially-insensitive-remarks/.
2. Lee Skallerup Bessette, "Tweets on Public Blogging (Screenshots on File with Author)," Twitter, March 5, 2014.
3. Nicholas Kristof, "Professors We Need You!" *New York Times*, February 15, 2014, https://perma.cc/EL3L-TD2H.
4. Corey Robin, "The Responsibility of Adjunct Intellectuals," *Al-Jazeera America*, March 12, 2014, http://america.aljazeera.com/opinions/2014/3/kristofacademicswritingpublicintellectuals.html.

4. On Writing

1. Rebecca Schuman, "Adjunct Heroics (Tweet on File with Author)," Twitter, January 31, 2014.
2. Sarah Kendzior, "What's the Point of Academic Publishing?" *Chronicle Vitae*, January 24, 2014, https://perma.cc/CTG3-P7KA.

6. Negative Capability

1. Cornel West, "Negative Capability (Tweet on File with the Author)," Twitter, June 21, 2011.
2. Kenneth L. Wainstein, "The Wainstein Report: Investigation of Irregular Classes in the Department of African and Afro-American Studies at the University of North Carolina at Chapel Hill" (Chapel Hill, N.C., October 16,

Notes

2014), https://carolinacommitment.unc.edu/wp-content/uploads/sites/350/2014/10/UNC-FINAL-REPORT.pdf.
3. University of North Carolina Residence Hall Association, "University of North Carolina Residence Hall Renaming Timeline," University of North Carolina at Chapel Hill, 2022, https://rha.unc.edu/renaming/#.
4. Louis Brandeis, "What Publicity Can Do," *Harper's Weekly*, December 20, 1913, https://perma.cc/V8N4-42DT.
5. Raul Pacheco-Vega, "Adjacent to Academia (Tweet on File with the Author)," Twitter, January 4, 2017.

7. Losing My Affiliation

1. American Presidency Project, "Vice Presidential Debate of 1992 in Atlanta Georgia: Senator Al Gore, Vice Admiral James Stockdale, Ross Perot," University of California at Santa Barbara, October 13, 1992, https://perma.cc/MD84-KB9L.

8. Reason to Believe

1. Susan Nolen-Hoeksema, Blair E. Wisco, and Sonja Lyubomirsky, "Rethinking Rumination," *Perspectives on Psychological Science* 3, no. 5 (September 2008): 400–424, https://doi.org/10.1111/j.1745-6924.2008.00088.x.
2. Bruce Springsteen, *Reason to Believe (Song)* (Columbia Records, 1982).

9. Bridging Academia

1. Raul Pacheco-Vega, "Adjacent to Academia (Tweet on File with the Author)," Twitter, January 4, 2017.

10. Quit Lit Is About Labor Conditions

1. Rebecca Schuman, "Thesis Hatement," *Slate*, April 5, 2013, https://perma.cc/YPP6-WRY4.
2. Kelly J. Baker, *Sexism Ed: Essays on Gender and Labor in Academia* (Chapel Hill, N.C.: Blue Crow Books, 2018).
3. Leonard Cassuto, "The Grief of the Ex-Academic," *The Chronicle of Higher Education*, February 25, 2018, https://perma.cc/83HQ-KUZW.
4. Sarah Brown, "She Wrote a Farewell Letter to Colleagues. Then 80,000 People Read It," *The Chronicle of Higher Education*, February 15, 2018, https://perma.cc/UZ8B-NJXT.
5. Annemarie Pérez, "Instead of Gaslighting Adjuncts, We Could Help Them," The Chronicle of Higher Education, April 15, 2018, https://perma.cc/6BN5-2G6R.

Notes

11. The University Is Just Another Client

1. Rebecca Schuman, "Adjunct Heroics (Tweet on File with Author)," Twitter, January 31, 2014.
2. Rebecca Schuman, "Hanging Up on a Calling," *The Chronicle of Higher Education*, January 27, 2014, https://perma.cc/N593-7BSG.
3. Rachel Leventhal-Wiener, "Don't Fear the Resume," *Chronicle Vitae*, Aug. 26, 2014, https://perma.cc/UB5E-F77P.

12. The Ugly Side of Academia

1. James Baldwin, "The Black Boy Looks at the White Boy," *Equire*, May 1961, 102.

13. The Invisible Adjunct Hero at Kentucky

1. Christopher Mele, "Student Arrested After Crawling Into a Duct to Steal an Exam," *New York Times*, May 4, 2017, https://perma.cc/872D-QCV2.
2. *Bull Durham* (Orion Pictures, 1988).

14. The Racism False Equivalence Strikes Again

1. Monterey County Herald, "NJ College: Professor Fired for Making Racially Insensitive Remarks," *Monterey County Herald*, June 24, 2017, https://perma.cc/287K-NHQM.
2. Supreme Court of the United States, Plessy v. Ferguson, 163 U.S. 537 (1896).
3. Tressie McMillan Cottom, "Everything But The Burden: Publics, Public Scholarship, And Institutions," *Some of Us Are Brave: The Archive*, May 12, 2015, https://perma.cc/2MUQ-DZYY.

15. What's Your BATNA?

1. Roger Fisher, William Ury, and Bruce Patton, *Getting to Yes: Negotiating Agreement Without Giving In*, 3rd ed. (New York: Penguin Books, 2011).
2. David Venter, "BATNA Explained," *The Negotiation Academy*, accessed June 6, 2024, https://perma.cc/A2XL-9D74.
3. Guhan Subramanian, "What Is BATNA? How to Find Your Best Alternative to a Negotiated Agreement," *Harvard Law School Program on Negotiation Blog*, May 2, 2024, https://perma.cc/69HC-HSL5.
4. Rebecca Schuman, "Adjunct Heroics (Tweet on File with Author)," Twitter, January 31, 2014.

Notes

16. Leaving a Legacy Off the Tenure Track

1. Edward L. Deci, "Effects of Externally Mediated Rewards on Intrinsic Motivation," *Journal of Personality and Social Psychology* 18, no. 1 (1971): 105–15.
2. Harry F. Harlow, Margaret Kuenne Harlow, and Donald R. Meyer, "Learning Motivated By A Manipulation Drive," *Journal of Experimental Psychology* 40, no. 2 (April 1950): 228–34, https://doi.org/10.1037%2Fh0056906.
3. Kelly J. Baker, "Academic Waste," *Chronicle Vitae*, February 23, 2016, https://perma.cc/A79T-PARW.
4. Nathaniel Koloc, "Build a Career Worth Having," *Harvard Business Review*, August 5, 2013, https://perma.cc/D4ZS-QG7M.

17. Why Attend Conferences as a Freelance Academic?

1. Kelly J. Baker, "What Can Learned Societies Do About Adjuncts," *Chronicle Vitae*, Jan. 5, 2015, https://perma.cc/QT6T-P8Q7.

18. Why Am I Teaching Again?

1. *Never Say Never Again* (Warner Bros., 1983).
2. Anne Lamott, Bird by Bird: Some Instructions on Writing and Life (New York: Anchor, 1994).

19. Launch Your Career Like James Bond

1. *Dr. No* (United Artists, 1962).

20. How to Start Working for Yourself

1. Sara Horowitz, "Why Freelancers Need a Nonpayment Law," *Fast Company*, January 28, 2016, https://perma.cc/TMS3-T4K4.
2. *Office Space* (20th Century Fox, 1999).

23. But I'm Still In Higher Ed

1. Megan, Interview with "Megan" regarding adjuncts and independent contractor status (real name on file with author), Email, March 31, 2015.
2. Kathleen DeLaney Thomas, Interview with Kathleen DeLaney Thomas regarding adjunct law, Email, May 15, 2015.
3. United States Tax Court, Schramm v. Commissioner, T.C. Memo. 2011-212 (2011).

Notes

24. It's Not Personal. It's Strictly Business

1. *The Godfather* (Paramount Pictures, 1972).

26. So You Want to Be a Freelance Writer

1. Liz Koblyk, "Instead of Trying to Satisfy All of Your Interests With One Job, Consider Compartmentalizing.," *University Affairs (Canada)*, April 10, 2017, https://perma.cc/3Q5N-5PLN.
2. Katie Rose Pryal, *Entanglement: A Hollywood Lights Novel* (Chapel Hill, N.C.: Blue Crow Books, 2015).
3. John Warner, "Volunteer Faculty: The Death Knell for Public Higher Ed," April 25, 2018, https://perma.cc/8TL7-EPMA.

27. Ten Questions Every Academic Should Ask Before Writing for the Public

1. Sarah E. Bond and Kevin Gannon, "Public Writing and the Junior Scholar," The Chronicle of Higher Education, October 15, 2019, https://perma.cc/4HJL-DUCK.
2. Colleen Flaherty, "Threats for What She Didn't Say," Inside Higher Ed, accessed August 16, 2024, https://perma.cc/QJD8-BT7F.
3. Tressie McMillan Cottom, "Everything But The Burden: Publics, Public Scholarship, And Institutions," *Some of Us Are Brave: The Archive*, May 12, 2015, https://perma.cc/2MUQ-DZYY.
4. Kecia Ali, *The Woman Question in Islamic Studies* (Princeton, NJ: Princeton University Press, 2024).
5. Christen A. Smith et al., "Cite Black Women: A Critical Praxis (A Statement)," *Feminist Anthropology* 2, no. 1 (2021): 10–17, https://doi.org/10.1002/fea2.12040.
6. Annie Dillard, *The Writing Life* (New York: Harper Perennial, 2013).

28. You Want to Write for the Public, but About What?

1. Kelly J. Baker, Interview with Kelly J. Baker about mistakes academics make when pitching stories, December 17, 2019.
2. Kevin Kruse, Interview with Kevin Kruse about mistakes academics make writing for the public, Email, December 20, 2019.
3. Sarah E. Bond, "Tips for Academics Transition to Public Scholarship," *Forbes.Com*, January 31, 2018, https://www.forbes.com/sites/drsarahbond/2018/01/31/vox-populi-tips-for-academics-transitioning-to-public-scholarship.

Notes

29. The Venue, the Pitch, and the Fee

1. Liz Bucar, Interview with Liz Bucar about public writing, Email, January 19, 2020.
2. Kelly J. Baker, "How to Craft a Pitch," *The Chronicle of Higher Education*, June 7, 2017, https://www.chronicle.com/article/how-to-craft-a-pitch.

30. Public Writing in Uncertain Times

1. Aaron Olver and Erin Celello, "I Nearly Died from H1N1. I Can Tell You This: Social Distancing Is the Best Potion We Have to Fight the Coronavirus in Wisconsin.," Milwaukee Journal Sentinel, April 23, 2020, https://perma.cc/4LDT-GEJJ.

31. How to Lose an Editor in Five Days

1. Evette Dionne, Interview with Evette Dionne about her preferences as an editor, Email, March 30, 2020.
2. Kelly J. Baker, Interview with Kelly J. Baker about her preferences as an editor, Email, March 29, 2020.

Acknowledgments

Acknowledgments to the Second Edition

In addition to the thanks below, I would like to thank Lauren Faulkenberry, Camille Pagán, and Kelly Harms for supporting this second edition and for believing in my work on mental health and neurodiversity. All of you are there for me when I need help staying on track and having faith in myself and my writing. And thank you to the editors and editorial assistants of this edition: Barbara Guest and A. Pryal.

Acknowledgments to the First Edition

Many people help make a book possible, and the same is true for this book, but perhaps even more true for this book. A freelancer is only a strong as the community who supports her, and I owe everything to mine.

I owe ideas to Sara Littlejohn, Brandy Grabow Brown, Greer McPhaden, Catherine Prendergast, and Tonya Ritola, my colleagues and friends who have sustained me through the years. Alexa Chew and Kelly J. Baker, in particular, have stood close when I needed support most.

I owe thanks to my coauthors Ruth McKinney, Jordynn Jack, and Alexa Chew, who have created books with me, which is an unbelievable feat, one that creates a relationship that lasts forever.

I owe thanks to my local community in Chapel Hill, including my favorite place to write, La Vita Dolce cafe, its owner Annie, and its manager Erin, who have always welcomed me. And now my local community includes so much of my family as well: my sister and her family, my aunts and uncles, and even my parents. I'm so glad we're all within shouting distance.

I owe thanks to my early mentors, Claire McGuire, Ann Garvin, and Gabriela Montell, without whom I wouldn't be writing this book at all.

Thanks to the editors and the magazines that first published early versions of some of the pages in this book: Sean Michael Morris at *Hybrid Pedagogy*, Kelly J. Baker at *Women in Higher Education*, and Gabriela Montell and Denise Magner at *The Chronicle of Higher Education*.

I owe thanks to the group I found as I first made my way as a freelance academic, who were always supportive and giving, in no particular order: Elizabeth Keenan, Sean Michael Morris, Rebecca Schuman, Raul Pacheco-Vega, Liana M. Silva, Annemarie Pérez, Kelly J. Baker, Jen Polk, Heidi Giusto, Lisa Munro, Lee Skallerup-Bessette, and Sarah Kendzior. I'm sure I'm forgetting a few of you, and I'm sorry.

I owe thanks to the Tall Poppy Writers, my women writers collective, who have supported me through the years, including the years of this transition from professor to writer. Ann Garvin, Camille Pagán, Kelly Harms, Amy Impellizzeri, Sonja Yoerg, Sandra Block, Amy Sue Nathan, Kelly Simmons, Susan Gloss, Janie Chang, and the rest of you amazing women—I'm so glad I can count on you.

I owe an immense debt of gratitude and friendship to Lauren Faulkenberry, my partner in this incredible business of writing and publishing—I wouldn't do it any other way.

And, as always, I thank my two children and my husband, who inspire me constantly.

About the Author

Katie Rose Pryal, J.D., Ph.D., is an award-winning author, keynote speaker, professor, and expert in mental health and neurodiversity.

She is the author of many books, including *Life of the Mind Interrupted: Essays on Mental Health and Disability in Higher Education* (Blue Osprey 2017), the IPPY-Gold-winning *Even If You're Broken: Bodies, Boundaries, and Mental Health* (Blue Osprey 2023, revised and expanded edition), and *A Light in the Tower: A New Reckoning with Mental Health in Higher Education* (University Press of Kansas 2024), winner of the 2024 IPPY Bronze Medal in Education.

She is also the author of the Hollywood Lights series of romantic women's fiction, which includes *Entanglement* and the IPPY-Gold-winning *Take Your Charming Somewhere Else*. Like all of Katie Pryal's writing, the series centers neurodiversity—in addition to angsty romance, star-crossed lovers, sexy woodworkers, movie stars, and happily-ever-afters.

She lives in Chapel Hill, North Carolina, with her spouse, children, and many, many animals. Visit her website, where you can read stories about her life and more, at katiepryal.com. Read her monthly letter on mental health and making the world a better place at pryalnews.com.

www.ingramcontent.com/pod-product-compliance
Lightning Source LLC
Chambersburg PA
CBHW060519080526
44586CB00012B/545